The Holy Psalms of David (Zabur) part two

The Holy Psalms of David (Zabur)

To all people of goodwill …

'I am convinced that humanity must learn to strive to hold to good relationships with all people, and to learn respect and empathy for those with whom we disagree. These two volumes are dedicated to building such relationships, based on a shared appreciation of the Psalms of David'
MJK

The Holy Psalms of David (Zabur) part two

by
Michael John Khan

Reflections and Poems based on the Psalms

The Holy Psalms of David, (Zabur)
Part two (Psalms 76-150)

Copyright Michael John Khan, 2021

All rights reserved

© ***Mikereflects***

Scripture quotations are taken from the Holy Bible, New Living Translation, copyright 1996, 2004 and used by permission of Tyndale House Publishers, Inc., Wheaton, Illinois 60189. All rights reserved.

ISBN: 9798745751523

Printed by Amazon.co.uk

PREFACE

I am well aware of the different understandings of a single Holy text that exist within a single religion (for myself, Christianity) let alone the different understandings of Scripture that exist between people of different religions. However, I am convinced that humanity must learn to strive to hold to good relationships with all people, and to learn respect and empathy for those with whom we disagree.

These two volumes of my reflections on the 'Psalms of David' are intended as a devotional aid to build individual relationship with God the Author of Life and to further empathy between people of different backgrounds.

Many of the Holy Psalms (Zabur in Arabic) were written as songs by the Hebrew King David (viz., Muslim prophet, Davud); some were written in times of stress others in times of personal reflection in his gratitude to God for saving him in times of trouble. Other psalms were written by devout Jews after David's reign and added to David's psalms to form written Holy Scripture for the last 2,500 years. The first translation of these Psalms was made from Hebrew to Greek following the conquest of the Middle East by Alexander the Great around 300 BCE.

I have included extracts from the Holy Bible New Living Translation (NLT), second edition (unless otherwise denoted) and occasionally I have added minor clarifications in brackets to suit context. However, I would encourage my readers to read the full text of the Psalms for themselves.
MJK

The Holy Psalms of David (Zabur)

THEMES

Glory of God, joy, worship & praise.

Creation Glory: Pslm 8, 19, 96, 104 139,

God's Greatness: Pslm 2, 8, 93, 106, 117, 145, 146

Joy & Worship: Pslm 1, 5, 9, 29, 40, 43, 63, 89, 92, 95, 96, 99, 100, 120, 126, 147, 145 to 150 incl.

Praise to God: Pslm 36, 47, 107, 114, 118, 134, 135

Messiah, Love of God, eternal life

Messiah: Psms 2, 8, 20, 22, 45, 47, 68, 89, 110, 111, 118

Love: Pslm 13, 23, 36, 43, 106, 107, 135, 106, 139

Eternal Life: Pslm 27, 46, 48, 102

Prayer, thanksgiving & repentance

Meditation: Pslm 1, 27, 37, 46, 131, 132

Prayer: Pslm, 32, 18, 62, 89, 90, 131, 138

Thankful: Pslm 9, 30, 34, 54, 100, 107, 136, 139, 147,150

Repent & Renewal: Pslm 50, 51, 65, 76, 80, 81, 85, 98

Forgiveness, grace, faithfulness, protection, guidance

Forgiveness: Pslm 24, 30, 103

Grace & Presence: Pslm 16, 17, 24, 37, 46, 71, 139

Protection & Guidance: Pslm 3, 11, 12, 23, 27, 32, 35, 34, 59, 60, 61, 86, 91, 102, 121, 125 128, 142,145

Faithfulness: Pslm 13, 16, 23, 105, 109, 115

Faith & Obedience: Pslm 28, 32, 33, 40, 43, 101, 116

Depressed, rejected, enemies, persecuted, God's word

Downcast: Pslm 22, 42, 43, 69, 77, 80, 143

Enemies & Evil: Pslm 3, 13, 71, 76, 79, 83, 124, 137, 140

Persecution: Pslm 7, 12, 28, 31, 55, 56, 79, 109, 123, 129

God's Word & fruit trees: Pslm 1, 19, 46, 119

Rebuke, leaders, training, history, justice & judgement
Fools & Rebuke: Pslm 2, 14, 53, 141
Leaders & Training: Pslm 72, 78, 82, 86, 119, 127
Royal (for State): Pslm 18, 76
History of Israel: Pslm 44, 105, 106
Justice: Pslm 7, 9, 11, 25, 26, 58, 67, 72, 94
Judgement: Pslm 5, 7, 9, 50, 53, 64, 73, 74, 75

Mercy, poor & needy, old age, righteousness, pilgrimage,
Mercy: Pslm 47, 130
Poor & Needy: Pslm 9, 10, 68, 113, 146
Old age: Pslm 71, 90
Righteousness: Pslm 4, 14, 15, 16, 34, 52, 89, 97
Sickness: Pslm 6, 30, 41
Sorrow: Pslm 3, 44, 77
Pilgrimage: Pslm 84, 120 to 134 incl.

Wisdom, unity, work, salvation, Zion and God's kingdom
Wisdom & Unity: Pslm 1, 37, 39, 49, 112, 143, 133
Work: Pslm 127, 144
Sin and sinners: Pslm 1, 14, 32, 38, 51, 69, 78, 120, 130
Salvation: Pslm 3, 24, 25, 51, 40, 49
Zion & God's Kingdom: Pslm 46, 48, 87, 97, 99, 102, 122

BOOKS & AUTHORS

The Five Books of Psalms

The 150 psalms in the Hebrew Bible (**Masoretic Text**) is divided into five "books", and each of the five concludes with a **doxology**: (*source accessed Wiki 2019: -: https://hermeneutics.stackexchange.com)*'

Book 1: Psalms 1—41 (doxology 41 v.13)

Book 2: Psalms 42—72 (doxology 72 v.18-19)

Book 3: Psalms 73—89 (doxology 106 v.52)

Book 4: Psalms 90—106 (doxology 106 v.48)

Book 5: Psalms 107—150 (doxology 150)

'It is uncertain why Psalms is divided into five books. Some sources, including Jewish Midrash traditions, suggest the five-fold division is based on the five books of the Torah (Genesis to Deuteronomy).'

Authors

'David is listed as the author of 73 psalms, Asaph of 12, and the sons of Korah of 11. Other psalms were written by Solomon, **Heman**, **Ethan** *and Moses. The earliest extant copy of Psalms is from the Dead Sea Scrolls from about the first century AD. That copy shows that the division into five books extends to at least that time and certainly earlier. It is most likely that* **Ezra** *and/or other Jewish religious leaders compiled the Psalms into their existing order in the fourth century BC. Interestingly, the Psalms was one of the most popular writings*

among the *Dead Sea Scrolls*, with thirty scrolls of all or parts of the book included. Overall, Psalms is the book of the Old Testament with the most Hebrew manuscripts available for research, indicating its enduring popularity among both Jews and Christians. Each of these five books or sections of Psalms ends with a doxology or a song of praise. The final verse of each concluding psalm includes either "Praise the Lord!" or "Amen." (Wikipedia, 2018).

I have written a brief commentary on selected extracts from each original psalm and added my own poems and prayers to each selection as well as provide the reader additional notes where I have deemed appropriate.

MJ Khan

Contents

INTRODUCTION	1
PSALM 76	3
PSALM 77	4
PSALM 78	5
PSALM 79	8
PSALM 80	10
PSALM 81	12
PSALM 82	14
PSALM 83	15
PSALM 84	16
PSALM 85	18
PSALM 86	20
PSALM 87	21
PSALM 88	22
PSALM 89	25
PSALM 90	27
PSALM 91	29
PSALM 92	31
PSALM 93	32
PSALM 94	33
PSALM 95	35
PSALM 96	36
PSALM 97	38
PSALM 98	39
PSALM 99	41

PSALM 100	43
PSALM 101	44
PSALM102	45
PSALM 103	47
PSALM 104	49
PSALM 105	52
PSALM 106	54
PSALM 107	56
PSALM 108	58
PSALM 109	59
PSALM 110	61
PSALM 111	63
PSALM 112	65
PSALM 113	66
PSALM 114	67
PSALM 115	68
PSALM 116	69
PSALM 117	70
PSALM 118	71
PSALM 119	73
PSALM 120	78
PSALM 121	79
PSALM 122	80
PSALM 123	81
PSALM 124	82
PSALM 125	82

PSALM 126	83
PSALM 127	85
PSALM 128	86
PSALM 129	87
PSALM 130	88
PSALM 131	90
PSALM 132	90
PSALM 133	93
PSALM 134	94
PSALM 135	95
PSALM 136	96
PSALM 137	97
PSALM 138	98
PSALM 139	99
PSALM 140	101
PSALM 141	103
PSALM 142	104
PSALM 143	105
PSALM 144	107
PSALM 145	108
PSALM 146	110
PSALM 147	111
PSALM 148	112
PSALM 149	114
PSALM 150	116
End Notes	117

INTRODUCTION

As life progresses, I increasingly notice that one of the most basic distinction between people in this world does not so much relate to a particular religious faith (e.g., Christianity, Islam, Judaism, etc.), nor between those who embrace a faith and those who don't (Agnostics, Atheists, etc.). Nor I see this basic distinction as between males and females, or between adults and children, or those blessed with intelligence and those not so blessed. The distinction I notice is between those who hold a world view that is rigidly 'cut and dried' and those whose hold their paradigms open to growth and development and see all of life as an adventure of discovery.

Let me clarify this; by 'cut and dried,' I mean those who can only embrace others on their own terms, whose view of reality and of those around them is so rigid that it is beyond correction, beyond development. And by 'those on an adventure' I mean those who are confident in their beliefs, but at the same time are open to exploration, un-conditionally embracing others, and open to the development of their belief systems. I think that those who are 'cut and dried' tend to be legalistic when it comes to religion (or atheism) and are more inclined to reject those who don't share their faith. And those who are adventurous possibly tend to have less self-righteousness and are a little more inclined to embrace God's mercy with faith and are more open to love and respect of those who hold different beliefs to themselves.

The psalms were written by King David and other godly people of the Hebrew/ Jewish faith that became Judaism. The Hebrews and Jews believed in the one God they called Yahweh (usually without the vowels since they did not like to speak his name). The Muslim prophet Muhammad first learnt about the 'One God' from Jewish traders to Arabia and became a believer and advocate of the One God against the backdrop of the pagan (polytheistic) Arab culture in which he was brought up. In Arabic the word used by both Muslim and Christian believers for God is

'Allah' (derived from the Semitic from El-aha or Al-aha). In Arabic there is no religious distinction in the use of this word 'Allah' for the One creator god. In English, however the word 'God' means the One creator god, and so when translating Allah into English for example, it is reasonable to use the word God and vice versa. I am aware however that this does present a problem for some people.

Christianity claims to be a development of Judaism that embraces the pre-Christian Jewish Scriptures[1] and as such the Christian concept of God is much the same as the Jewish concept, except that in Jesus Christ, Christians see God as intimate (a concept alien to the Jews) and immanent. Islam claims to be a development of both Judaism and Christianity however due to some negations of the pre-Islamic Jewish and Christian conceptions of God in the Qur'an and subsequent Islamic texts, Muslims, Christians and Jews do not see the 'One God' in quite the same light.

We must also note that the Psalms were written as poetry to be sung to music and as such although they are inspired by God's Spirit, nevertheless must be seen as inspiring faith to our spirits and emotions rather than necessarily conveying a literal truth. For space and copyright reasons I have not included the whole text of the psalms nor kept their poetic form, however, in recognition this limitation, I have sought to include a short poem of my own drawn from each psalm followed by a short prayer.

Although I write as a Christian, I trust these reflections will draw together those of good will from all faith backgrounds.

For further comment – please read my End Notes

---

[1] The archaeological find of the Dead Sea Scrolls has verified that the Hebrew scriptures have remained unchanged since first translated into Greek in around 300BCE

Introduction

PSALM 76[2]

'¹God's name is great in Israel. ² Jerusalem is where he lives; Mount Zion is his home. ³ There he has broken the fiery arrows of the enemy, the shields and swords and weapons of war.

⁴ You are glorious and more majestic than the everlasting mountains. ⁵ Our boldest enemies have been plundered. They lie before us in the sleep of death. No warrior could lift a hand against us. … ⁹ You stand up to judge those who do evil, O God, and to rescue the oppressed of the earth. ¹⁰ Human defiance only enhances your glory, for you use it as a weapon. ¹¹ Make vows to the LORD your God and keep them. Let everyone bring tribute to the Awesome One. ¹² For he breaks the pride of princes, and the kings of the earth fear him.'

This highly nationalistic psalm was written by the seer Asaph, and should not detract us from the fact that our creator God is Lord of all nations whether or not those nations acknowledge allegiance to God. Asaph's praise (v.9-10) is true for all peoples: our God is more glorious than the everlasting mountains and human defiance does enhance God's glory because human pride will always be brought down to the dust in time! *(v.2, see end notes)*.

We need to praise the God of all creation and encourage all people to worship God alone. The human pride Asaph speaks of in v.12 is that which stems from self-reliance rather than from a confidence based in humble submission to God's grace in our lives.

---

[2] (see Books & authors of the Psalms)

A poem based on Psalm 76: -
> O Lord God our maker,
> Your glory is greater
> than all the heavens;
> You bring all pride to dust,
> And rescue those who trust
> You, with their Amens!

A prayer: - Lord' lift the oppressed and give them joy! Amen

PSALM 77

This is another Psalm of Asaph pouring out his sorrow to God and renewing his faith.

[1] I cry out to God; yes, I shout. Oh, that God would listen to me! [2] When I was in deep trouble, I searched for the Lord. All night long I prayed, with hands lifted toward heaven, but my soul was not comforted. ... [5] I think of the good old days, long since ended, [6] when my nights were filled with joyful songs. I search my soul and ponder the difference now. [7] Has the Lord rejected me forever? Will he never again be kind to me? [8] Is his unfailing love gone forever? Have his promises permanently failed? [9] Has God forgotten to be gracious? Has he slammed the door on his compassion? ... [11] But then I recall all you have done, O LORD; I remember your wonderful deeds of long ago. [12] They are constantly in my thoughts. I cannot stop thinking about your mighty works.

There are times it seems we are banging on a closed door to no avail, when God seems far off. Things aren't going our way and our prayers are bouncing off the ceiling. But we need to ask ourselves, for whose benefit are we praying: ours or for God's glory? Are we willing for God to re-shape us so that we glorify him, or are we just wanting God to reshape our circumstances so we can continue the way we were?

Asaph showed how important it is to bring our complaints to God, and to remind ourselves of God's blessings and mercies especially when we feel God is far from us (v.9). In doing so, the psalmist began to renew his faith in God (v.11). We need to look to God not to change our circumstances so much as to change us to be more inline with his purposes, by learning to lean into God's love and trust God to work out his purpose in and through us.

A poem based on Psalm 77: -
I'm so distressed I can't pray!
What's going on God?
Why this disaster on us?
We're feeling your rod,
Don't slam the door in our face
Just give us a nod
Please just rescue all our thoughts.
Be our saviour, dear God!

A prayer: Forgive my sins, renew my faith! Amen

PSALM 78

Here is another psalm written by Asaph, this time reflecting Israel's history. Despite God's mighty acts in delivering them from slavery in Egypt, the people lacked faith and went through cycles of rebellion, punishment, repentance and restoration.

¹O my people, listen to my instructions. Open your ears to what I am saying,² for I will speak to you in a parable. I will teach you hidden lessons from our past— ³ stories we have heard and known, stories our ancestors handed down to us. ⁴ We will not hide these truths from our children; we will tell the next generation about the glorious deeds of the LORD ...

> ... ⁷ So each generation should set its hope anew on God, not forgetting his glorious miracles and obeying his commands. ⁸ Then they will not be like their ancestors— stubborn, rebellious, and unfaithful, refusing to give their hearts to God. ⁹ The warriors of Ephraim, though armed with bows, turned their backs and fled on the day of battle. ¹⁰ They did not keep God's covenant and refused to live by his instructions. ¹¹ They forgot what he had done— the great wonders he had shown them, ¹² the miracles he did for their ancestors on the plain of Zoan in the land of Egypt.

The Psalmist points to an example contemporary to the people of Israel whom he was addressing, and compared them to warriors of Ephraim who left the battle field and fled in a cowardly manner. Mercenaries don't fight to the death, because they are generally fighting for a cause they don't really believe in. Ephraim was one of the chosen tribes of Israel and the Psalmist knew that if they were really men of faith, living to defend their heritage, they should not have fed on the day of battle. When we are truly grateful to God for the blessings we have received, we will stand firm to defend God's honour. The Ephraimites fled because they lacked the courage that faith would have given them. They weren't grateful to the God of their heritage.

Asaph then launched into a lengthy parable describing how their ancestors like them had much to be grateful to God for, but had lacked faith despite God's faithfulness to them.

> ¹⁴ In the daytime he led them by a cloud, and all night by a pillar of fire. ¹⁵ He split open the rocks in the wilderness to give them water ...' ¹⁷ Yet they kept on sinning against him.... ¹⁸ They stubbornly tested God in their hearts, demanding the foods they craved. ¹⁹ They even spoke against God himself, ...²² for they did not believe God ... ²³ But he commanded the skies to open; he opened the doors of heaven.

Psalm 78

> [24] He rained down manna for them to eat; he gave them bread from heaven.
>
> [32] But in spite of this, the people kept sinning. Despite his wonders, they refused to trust him. [33] So he ended their lives in failure, their years in terror. [34] When God began killing them, they finally sought him. They repented and took God seriously. [35] Then they remembered that God was their rock, that God Most High was their redeemer. [36] But all they gave him was lip service; they lied to him with their tongues. [37] Their hearts were not loyal to him. They did not keep his covenant. [38] Yet he was merciful and forgave their sins and did not destroy them all. ... Many times, he held back his anger and did not unleash his fury! [39] For he remembered that they were merely mortal, gone like a breath of wind that never returns. ...

Asaph was gently calling the people of Israel back to faith in God, challenging them not to merely pay God lip-service but to wholeheartedly give themselves to worshiping God and being faithful to their promises. At the same time, he was warning them that being faithless would lead to terrible consequences. Are we faithless at times or merely paying lip-service to God? Or, are we trusting God for his grace through each day?

> [70] He chose his servant David, calling him from the sheep pens. [71] He took David from tending the ewes and lambs and made him the shepherd of Jacob's descendants— God's own people, Israel. [72] He cared for them with a true heart and led them with skilful hands.

Finally, Asaph pointed to God's salvation, pre-figured in the life of King David. For all people of faith in future generations this salvation is figured in David's greater son the heavenly king Jesus.

A poem drawn from Psalm 78: -

Comfortable in complacency,
Our hearts are cold and unclean.
We fail to live 'good news' each day:
So, your relevance is unseen!
We your people have been faithless,
Paying lip service to you.
Put your Spirit into us we pray.
What you promised in us do!
But thank you God your work depends,
Not on us, but on what you do.
So, working faith in all our hearts
Bring our nation back to you.

A prayer: - Turn our nation back to you we pray and save our souls. Amen

PSALM 79

¹ O God, pagan nations have conquered your land, your special possession. They have defiled your holy Temple and made Jerusalem a heap of ruins. ² They have left the bodies of your servants as food for the birds of heaven …. ⁴ We are mocked by our neighbours, an object of scorn and derision to those around us.

This song of Asaph tells of a time when Jerusalem had been overrun and its inhabitants slaughtered. The godly despaired: God had abandoned them. And as is common to humanity they felt that their loss must be because of sin. However, the Scriptures tell us that loss is not necessarily due to sin.

⁵ O LORD, how long will you be angry with us? Forever? How long will your jealousy burn like fire? ⁶ Pour out your wrath on the nations that refuse to acknowledge you— on kingdoms that do not call upon your name.

> **⁷ For they have devoured your people Israel, making the land a desolate wilderness. ⁸ Do not hold us guilty for the sins of our ancestors! Let your compassion quickly meet our needs, for we are on the brink of despair. ...**

God allows bad things to happen even to his dearest people. We are however assured that if we lean on God, we will be comforted and strengthened to endure and to demonstrate God's great love for humanity and his patience with sinners!

> **¹² O Lord, pay back our neighbours seven times for the scorn they have hurled at you. ¹³ Then we your people, the sheep of your pasture, will thank you forever and ever, praising your greatness from generation to generation.**

Asaph goes on to pray for God's vengeance on Israel's enemies. However, the greatest Jewish Israelite, the Messiah Jesus Christ came not to bring vengeance but to **'demonstrate God's mercy on us even while we were still lost in sin'** and even to **'give his life as a ransom for many.'** Yes, Jesus was and is the ultimate 'face of the Creator God' showing that God is very patient and loves even our enemies and would see them repent and find his favour rather than die and perish.

A Poem from Psalm 79: -
> *God, I confess to you*
> *My sorrow, my distress.*
> *We are treated like pigs*
> *Despite our righteousness.*
> *Our enemies don't care*
> *About any godliness.*
> *Have you abandoned us?*
> *Left us in our distress?*
> *No! Your promise is sure*
> *You will never leave us!*

Replace our vengeful thoughts,
Put your Spirit in us:
To love our enemies,
To pay back good for ill,
To show your loving care,
To love and not to kill!

A prayer: Lord put you love in my heart in place of anger and vengeance. Amen

PSALM 80

This Psalm by Asaph is prayer for revival to God after lands had been lost, and the people decimated.

[1] Please listen, O Shepherd of Israel, you who lead Joseph's descendants like a flock. O God, enthroned above the cherubim, display your radiant glory [2] to Ephraim, Benjamin, and Manasseh. Show us your mighty power. Come to rescue us! [3] Turn us again to yourself, O God. Make your face shine down upon us. Only then will we be saved. [4] O LORD God of Heaven's Armies, how long will you be angry with our prayers? [5] You have fed us with sorrow and made us drink tears by the bucketful. ... [8] You brought us from Egypt like a grapevine; you drove away the pagan nations and transplanted us into your land. [9] You cleared the ground for us, and we took root and filled the land. [10] Our shade covered the mountains; our branches covered the mighty cedars. ... [12] But now, why have you broken down our walls so that all who pass by may steal our fruit? ....

There is an assumption in this psalm that the God of creation, the God of Abraham and Moses, would come to their rescue if they prayed. But there is no mention here of sin or confession of waywardness.

However, verse 3 implies that the nation needed to be turned towards God. As Jesus taught (Jn.16 v.9), all those who don't live each day trusting in God and following his way are in a state of rebellion against God.

Asaph was appealing to God's nature to bring about God's purpose for his nation. He may have been holding onto the promise of God to bless the nations of the world through Abraham's faithful offspring (the Messiah), but God expects his people to repent of their sins before God can revive them.

[14] Come back, we beg you, O God of Heaven's Armies. Look down from heaven and see our plight. Take care of this grapevine[15] that you yourself have planted, this son you have raised for yourself. [16] For we are chopped up and burned by our enemies. May they perish at the sight of your frown. [17] Strengthen the man you love, the son of your choice. [18] Then we will never abandon you again. Revive us so we can call on your name once more. [19] Turn us again to yourself, O LORD God of Heaven's Armies. Make your face shine down upon us. Only then will we be saved.

Asaph along with other OT authors saw the nation as God's precious grapevine – his hope was that having allowed the old wood to be chopped down and burned, God would revive the faith roots of the nation and would then nurture and protect the new growth. How much do we encourage our youth to experience God for themselves and to follow the new paths God leads them on, and to expect God to act through them?

A poem based on Psalm 80: -

> *Lord God we have believed that*
> *It was you who led us to victory,*
> *That it was your love that gave us our land.*
> *But now we are chopped down and*
> *Burned by our enemies, we look to you:*
> *Have you abandoned us - broken our walls?*

Psalm 80

Lord we believe in your love,
That we are your precious vine: turn to us,
Revive us again so that we can pray.
So, let your face shine on us
That we turn to you and confess our sin
Please send us your Spirit to guide our way
And save us from ourselves. Amen

A prayer: Lord I confess my waywardness, please show me your way.

PSALM 81

This was another of Asaph's psalms originally written to be sung to the music of stringed instruments.

The psalm is a call to worship. It is good to give thanks to God at all times as well as at special times! The psalmist recounts how God saved his ancestors from slavery in Egypt. The words translated as an 'unknown voice (v.5b)' may possibly be meant as 'the unfamiliar voice of God', i.e., inferring that the people of Israel were not used to listening out for the voice of God

¹ Sing praises to God, our strength. Sing to the God of Jacob. ² Sing! Beat the tambourine. Play the sweet lyre and the harp. ³ Blow the ram's horn at new moon, and again at full moon to call a festival! ⁴ For this is required by the decrees of Israel; it is a regulation of the God of Jacob. ... ⁵ᵇ"I heard an unknown voice say, ⁶ "Now I will take the load from your shoulders; I will free your hands from their heavy tasks. ⁷ You cried to me in trouble, and I saved you; I answered out of the thundercloud and tested your faith when there was no water at Meribah (*In the Sinai desert)* ⁸ "Listen to me, O my people, while I give you stern warnings. O Israel, if you would only listen to me! ⁹ You must never have a foreign god; you must not bow down before a false god.

¹⁰ For it was I, the LORD your God, who rescued you from the land of Egypt. Open your mouth wide, and I will fill it with good things.

The people of Israel nevertheless did turn to false gods and worship them. Do we not also from time to time worship the false gods of 'commercialism', 'pleasure,' and 'self-justification'?

¹¹ "But no, my people wouldn't listen. Israel did not want me around. ¹² So I let them follow their own stubborn desires, living according to their own ideas. ¹³ Oh, that my people would listen to me! Oh, that Israel would follow me, walking in my paths! ¹⁴ How quickly I would then subdue their enemies! How soon my hands would be upon their foes! ... ¹⁶ But I would feed you with the finest wheat. I would satisfy you with wild honey from the rock."

Here God promises that he will prove faithful when his people put God first in their lives. The same is true for us when we seek God's face and walk humbly with our God!

A poem derived from psalm 81: -

In the desert the people moaned
Testing God not thanking him
For the blessings they had received.
How we too easily moan dear Lord!
When the going is too tough,
We fail to trust, and you are grieved.
Help us to praise you at all times
You are always there for us
And by our faith you are perceived!

A prayer: Help us to trust and praise you and not faint.

PSALM 82

[1] God presides over heaven's court; he pronounces judgment on the heavenly beings: [2] "How long will you hand down unjust decisions by favouring the wicked? [3] Give justice to the poor and the orphan; uphold the rights of the oppressed and the destitute. [4] Rescue the poor and helpless; deliver them from the grasp of evil people. [5] But these oppressors know nothing; they are so ignorant! They wander about in darkness, while the whole world is shaken to the core. [6] I say, 'You are gods; you are all children of the Most-High. [7] But you will die like mere mortals and fall like every other ruler.'"

Although Scripture does speak of the 'cosmic powers of darkness', it is clear from the context here, that the Asaph was using hyperbole and sarcasm to face the corrupt leaders of his nation with their partiality when exercising justice. Since the Psalmist believed that God is just and upholds justice for all, he imagined a scene where God is sitting in judgement on those earthly leaders who are themselves responsible for justice on earth but are abjectly failing to apply God's standards. And the Psalmist prophetically spoke to such unjust leaders reminding them that although they behaved as if they were gods, and were created by Almighty God, they would one day perish as all mortals do!

[8] Rise up, O God, and judge the earth, for all the nations belong to you.

The Psalmist then appealed to the God of justice to bring justice into all nations. This is a very worthy prayer. The fact that the Psalmist looked beyond his own nation into all the world showed an amazing appreciation of God's love for the whole planet. We should also be inspired to look beyond our own kith and kin to seek social justice for all peoples as well as environmental justice for earth's eco-systems and creatures.

Psalm 84

A poem from Psalm 82: -

> *Lord God our rulers continually fail*
> *To press for justice small and wide*
> *To save the weak and trodden-down*
> *To prevent the careless wonton misuse*
> *Of earth's resources or the abuse of souls.*
> *Come Holy Spirit inspire us all*
> *To cloth ourselves in God's own grace*
> *To stand up against all tyrants now*
> *And face them down in your power!*

A prayer: Lord God help me be brave trusting in your grace. Amen.

PSALM 83

'¹O God, do not be silent! ... ²Don't you hear the uproar of your enemies? Don't you see that your arrogant enemies are rising up? ³They devise crafty schemes against your people; they conspire against your precious ones. ⁴"Come," they say, "let us wipe out Israel as a nation. We will destroy the very memory of its existence." ⁵Yes, this was their unanimous decision. They signed a treaty as allies against you ...'

¹³O my God, scatter them like tumbleweed, like chaff before the wind! ¹⁴As a fire burns a forest and as a flame sets mountains ablaze, ¹⁵chase them with your fierce storm; terrify them with your tempest. ¹⁶Utterly disgrace them until they submit to your name, O Lord. ¹⁷Let them be ashamed and terrified forever. Let them die in disgrace. ¹⁸Then they will learn that you alone are called the Lord, that you alone are the Most High, supreme over all the earth.

Asaph's people were primarily God's people, so he expected God to defend them. He was unabashed to tell God what he expected God to do; however, his love for God was such that he wanted his enemies to learn to submit to the one true God (v.18). When we pray, do we pray with passion? If we don't, could it be because we aren't so confident in our relationship with God? And when we pray, do we pray seeking the furtherance of God's rule in the hearts of all others, or are we merely looking to further our own agendas?

A poem drawn from Psalm 83: -

> *God, I know you really love me*
> *May your heart fill mine with passion,*
> *That I will beg you on my knees,*
> *Other lives to bring to know you*
> *And by grace that I so love you*
> *That they will follow your decrees.*

A prayer: Lord God, help me to love you better. Amen

PSALM 84

Written by the musical descendants of Korah.

¹ How lovely is your dwelling place, O Lord of Heaven's Armies. ² I long, yes, I faint with longing to enter the courts of the Lord. With my whole being, body and soul, I will shout joyfully to the living God. ³ Even the sparrow finds a home, and the swallow builds her nest and raises her young at a place near your altar, O Lord of Heaven's Armies, my King and my God! ⁴ What joy for those who can live in your house, always singing your praises.

The psalm was written for pilgrims to sing as they journeyed to the Jerusalem temple. There can be a comradery and bonding when we make regular pilgrimages or holidays either with family or friends or both. At another level we can aspire to both the temporal and eternal joy of God's presence now and for eternity. Pilgrimages and holidays can be a time when we draw near to God in new and refreshing ways that provide a break from the on-going call to live out our faith in the heat and sweat of the world around us.

5 What joy for those whose strength comes from the Lord, who have set their minds on a pilgrimage to Jerusalem. 6 When they walk through the Valley of Weeping, it will become a place of refreshing springs. The autumn rains will clothe it with blessings. 7 They will continue to grow stronger, and each of them will appear before God in Jerusalem. 8 O Lord God of Heaven's Armies, hear my prayer. Listen, O God of Jacob.

Those who fully trust in their God will know his peace in their minds and hearts and find his strength even in times of conflict and trial. The very stones in their path will be turned to refreshing water through God's grace welling up within them.

9 O God, look with favour upon the king, our shield! Show favour to the one you have anointed. 10 A single day in your courts is better than a thousand anywhere else! I would rather be a gatekeeper in the house of my God than live the good life in the homes of the wicked. 11 For the Lord God is our sun and our shield. He gives us grace and glory. The Lord will withhold no good thing from those who do what is right. 12 O Lord of Heaven's Armies, what joy for those who trust in you.

There is a sure promise here for those whose faith is in the Lord God. God is good and he does not withhold any good thing from those who walk in faith and trust in God.

A poem based on Psalm 84: -

> *Lord I long to sing joyfully in your presence,*
> *When all conflict will cease:*
> *To be wholly at one with my friends and know that*
> *My heart is then at peace.*

A prayer: Lord be my peace as I trust in you each day. Amen

PSALM 85

Another psalm from Korah's descendants.

¹ Lord, you poured out blessings on your land! You restored the fortunes of Israel. ² You forgave the guilt of your people—yes, you covered all their sins. ³ You held back your fury. You kept back your blazing anger. ⁴ Now restore us again, O God of our salvation. Put aside your anger against us once more. ⁵ Will you be angry with us always? Will you prolong your wrath to all generations? ⁶ Won't you revive us again, so your people can rejoice in you? ⁷ Show us your unfailing love, O Lord, and grant us your salvation.

The Psalmist started his prayer (verses 1-3) by thankfully reminding God of his past mercy on the guilty nation. It then likely that Israel had been defeated in battle and the Psalmist while acknowledging the sin of the people, was (verse 4-7) pleading for God's mercy again on his nation.

Unlike the god of any other religion, the God of the Holy Bible (Torah, Prophets, Zabur and Ingil) is the God who forgives sins. God 'covers the sins (v.2)' of those who trust and follow him and he forgives their guilt! They can never earn God's forgiveness – only God can wipe out their sins, not by ignoring them or whitewashing over them – but by God himself facing the reality of their sin head on by his own self-sacrificing eternal love.

⁸ I listen carefully to what God the Lord is saying, for he speaks peace to his faithful people. But let them not return to their foolish ways. ⁹ Surely his salvation is near to those who fear him, so our land will be filled with his glory.

¹⁰ Unfailing love and truth have met together. Righteousness and peace have kissed! ¹¹ Truth springs up from the earth, and righteousness smiles down from heaven. ¹² Yes, the Lord pours down his blessings. Our land will yield its bountiful harvest. ¹³ Righteousness goes as a herald before him, preparing the way for his steps.

But love calls to love! God can and will create a clean heart in us. God's love calls out a loving response from us sinful creatures. We can experience God's forging love and grace for ourselves. We can experience joy, re-instatement, belonging, love, but only with a humble and dependent heart; dependent on God's ongoing grace and Spirit day by day hour by hour.

A poem from Psalm 85: -

> *God of Abraham and Jesus*
> *Your love poured out is undeserved,*
> *Forgive our sin and heal our land*
> *Our love responds, and you are glad!*

A prayer: We are like sheep – shepherd us with your rod.
Amen

PSALM 86

[1] Bend down, O Lord, and hear my prayer; answer me, for I need your help. [2] Protect me, for I am devoted to you. Save me, for I serve you and trust you. You are my God. [3] Be merciful to me, O Lord, for I am calling on you constantly. [4] Give me happiness, O Lord, for I give myself to you. [5] O Lord, you are so good, so ready to forgive, so full of unfailing love for all who ask for your help. [6] Listen closely to my prayer, O Lord; hear my urgent cry. [7] I will call to you whenever I'm in trouble, and you will answer me.

[8] No pagan god is like you, O Lord. None can do what you do! [9] All the nations you made will come and bow before you, Lord; they will praise your holy name. [10] For you are great and perform wonderful deeds. You alone are God.

[11] Teach me your ways, O Lord, that I may live according to your truth! Grant me purity of heart, so that I may honour you. [12] With all my heart I will praise you, O Lord my God. I will give glory to your name forever, [13] for your love for me is very great. You have rescued me from the depths of death. [14] O God, insolent people rise up against me; a violent gang is trying to kill me. You mean nothing to them. [15] But you, O Lord, are a God of compassion and mercy, slow to get angry and filled with unfailing love and faithfulness. [16] Look down and have mercy on me. Give your strength to your servant; save me, the son of your servant. [17] Send me a sign of your favour. Then those who hate me will be put to shame, for you, O Lord, help and comfort me.

A poem: -

Great is the Lord, greatly to be praised
His ways are filled with mercy from above.
He rescues those who depend on him
And he indwells them with his Christ of love

A Prayer: O God I depend on you. You receive me as I receive your truth, forgiveness and love. Amen

PSALM 87

A psalm of the descendants of Korah.

'1 On the holy mountain stands the city founded by the Lord. 2 He loves the city of Jerusalem more than any other city in Israel. O city of God, what glorious things are said about you!'

Jerusalem has inspired many a song such as 'Glorious things of thee are spoken, Zion city of our God' (a Christian hymn) and many others. The NT (Ingil) book of Revelation speaks of God bringing down the new Jerusalem following the final Judgement Day when the book of life is opened,

'And I saw the holy city, the new Jerusalem, coming down from God out of heaven like a bride beautifully dressed for her husband (Rev.21 v.2)'

It is clear that in the Psalms and many other Scriptures that the earthly city of Jerusalem holds a symbolic context which is sacred to Jews, Muslims and Christians. It is a symbol of where those who live by the kind of faith displayed by Abraham, will dwell with God in eternity. It represents the gaol of true faith in God.

The psalmist continues:

'4 I will count Egypt and Babylon (Iraq) among those who know me – also Philistia and Tyre, and even distant Ethiopia. They have all become citizens of Jerusalem! 5 Regarding Jerusalem it will be said, "Everyone enjoys the rights of citizenship there." ... 6 When the Lord registers the nations, he will say, "They have all become citizens of Jerusalem"' '7 The people will dance and sing, "The source of my life springs from Jerusalem!"'

The psalmist's vision is lifted from neighbouring nations he was aware of (v.4) to all the nations of the world (v.6) as he is inspired to realise that there will be those from every nation on earth who will enjoy God's eternal presence in the new Jerusalem following the final judgement when 'God registers the nations.' They will have become citizens of 'eternal life' and their faith will be realised in the worship of God based on God's presence and love permeating their whole beings. The psalmist concludes with the joy of those who receive the eternal life God offers to all.

A poem based on Psalm 87: -

Happy the day when all are gathered
Who lived by faith - they will dance and sing;
In God's presence filled with His love
Praise to their God their worship will bring.
The eternal God does welcome all
Who leave behind all the pull of earth,
For the godly love their Lord to share:
They will receive from him re-birth!

A prayer: Dear God help me ever hope in you and seek to praise you. Amen.

PSALM 88

A psalm written by Heman one of the descendants of Korah who in suffering much affliction felt abandoned by God.

Sadly, there are many in this world who are born into affliction through no fault of their own, suffering physical ailments, poverty, the prejudice of others, the stigma of birth, or the persecution of race, or gender or religion, and some may well feel as Heman felt despite his having faith in God.

¹ O Lord, God of my salvation, I cry out to you by day. I come to you at night. ... ³ For my life is full of troubles, and death draws near. ⁴ I am as good as dead, like a strong man with no strength left. ⁵ They have left me among the dead, and I lie like a corpse in a grave. I am forgotten, cut off from your care. ⁶ You have thrown me into the lowest pit, into the darkest depths. ⁷ Your anger weighs me down; with wave after wave you have engulfed me.

⁸ You have driven my friends away by making me repulsive to them. I am in a trap with no way of escape. ⁹ My eyes are blinded by my tears. Each day I beg for your help, O Lord; I lift my hands to you for mercy. ¹⁰ Are your wonderful deeds of any use to the dead? Do the dead rise up and praise you?

¹¹ Can those in the grave declare your unfailing love? Can they proclaim your faithfulness in the place of destruction? ¹² Can the darkness speak of your wonderful deeds? Can anyone in the land of forgetfulness talk about your righteousness? ¹³ O Lord, I cry out to you. I will keep on pleading day by day. ¹⁴ O Lord, why do you reject me? Why do you turn your face from me?

¹⁵ I have been sick and close to death since my youth. I stand helpless and desperate before your terrors. ¹⁶ Your fierce anger has overwhelmed me. Your terrors have paralyzed me. ¹⁷ They swirl around me like floodwaters all day long. They have engulfed me completely. ¹⁸ You have taken away my companions and loved ones. Darkness is my closest friend.

Some who lack the security of a wholesome life, can become bitter, dismissive of authority (which may have let them down) and aggressive. Some cry out to God in desperation while others despair of hope, or turn to drugs or crime as opportunity may arise. They may blame God for their lot in life, claiming that if God exists, then God must be responsible. Others blame their un-sociable actions or behaviour on their up-bringing or their genes. However, some will hold onto hope and develop their faith in God.

Heman could be alluding to dementia sufferers in verse 12, and in verses 8 and 18 speaks of being bereft of friendship. This is one of the most debilitating aspects of life people can face. The Lord God says, 'It is not good for man to be alone (Genesis 2 v.18)'. People who fear for their reputation, suffer depression, or are bereft of friendship, can find that darkness swallows them up, and feel with the Psalmist that, 'Darkness is my closest friend! (v.18)'

In verses 11-14, Heman argues that it would be better that God rescue him and give him a voice on earth so he could proclaim God's goodness to all, rather than leaving him to languish in his present state. However, scripture bids us to seek and find God's grace in all our circumstances – then our outlook will glorify God despite our troubles.

A poem inspired by Heman's Psalm 88

Darkness is my closest friend
Lord God I am bereft. I blame you!
From childhood I have been abandoned.
This life is not fair and you're to blame I feel.
But I will not despair! I will hope in you
To rescue me, to give me hope
And secure this my shrinking island
Before I am washed away!

A prayer: Lord God may my trust and hope be in you all my days. Amen

PSALM 89

This psalm is said to have been composed by a descendent of one of King David's loyal warriors, Ethan the Ezrahite.

The psalm elaborates on a prophesy (v.20-27) about David made by the prophet Nathan (2 Sam 7 v.12-17). It was written at a time when the prophesy was distant memory and the house of David despised. The writer starts by praising God.

'[1] I will sing of the LORD's unfailing love forever! Young and old will hear of your faithfulness. [2] Your unfailing love will last forever. ... [7] The highest angelic powers stand in awe of God. He is far more awesome than all who surround his throne. [8] O LORD God of Heaven's Armies! ... Your right hand is lifted high in glorious strength. ... [14] Righteousness and justice are the foundation of your throne. Unfailing love and truth walk before you as attendants. [15] Happy are those who hear the joyful call to worship, for they will walk in the light of your presence, LORD. [16] They rejoice all day long in your wonderful reputation. They exult in your righteousness. [17] You are their glorious strength. It pleases you to make us strong. [18] Yes, our protection comes from the LORD, and he, the Holy One of Israel, has given us our king.'

If the commentators are right and this was written in a time of great national trial, then it reminds us that it is always right to seek to praise God in whatever circumstances we find ourselves.

'[19] Long ago you spoke in a vision to your faithful people. You said, "I have raised up a warrior. I have selected him from the common people to be king. [20] I have found my servant David. I have anointed him with my holy oil. [21] I will steady him with my hand; ...[26] And he will call out to me, 'You are my Father, my God, and the Rock of my salvation.' [27] I will make him my firstborn son, the mightiest king on earth. [28] I will love him and be kind to him forever; my covenant with him will never end. ²⁹ I will preserve an heir for him; his throne will be as endless as the days of heaven. ... ³⁴ No, I will not break my covenant; I will not take back a single word I said. ³⁵ I have sworn an oath to David, and in my holiness, I cannot lie: ³⁶ His dynasty will go on forever; his kingdom will endure as the sun ...!"

Clearly this elaboration of prophesy *(see end note)* does not relate to King David's earthly dynasty which didn't last long at all, but rather it was given by God's Spirit in relation to the wider OT prophesy relating to David's greater son, the Messiah who would represent God's relationship with humanity for all time. It is the dynasty of faith that endures: Isaiah and other prophets spoke clearly of this (e.g., Is.52-55).

⁴⁹'You promised it to David with a faithful pledge. ⁵⁰ Consider, Lord, how your servants are disgraced! I carry in my heart the insults of so many people. ⁵¹ Your enemies have mocked me, O LORD; they mock your anointed king wherever he goes. ⁵² Praise the LORD forever! Amen and amen!'

And yet here the psalmist brings to God the pitiful state of David's dynastic descendent, hoping and praying that God will restore the earthly dynasty of Israel. It is right to pray for our country and leaders, while remembering that what really matters is our people's response to God's love for them demonstrated through David's greater son, God's Messiah, Jesus Christ.

A poem on this theme: -
I will praise you God each and every day:
'You are good and Your presence I will seek!'
The godless besiege us, yet we will praise you!
Help us show your love each and every day
To all regardless just as you pour out
Your rain and sunshine on good and bad alike!

A prayer: Lord give me strength for this day. Amen

PSALM 90[3]

'A prayer of Moses, the man of God.'

Said to be a psalm written by Moses as he led the people in the wilderness after they had sinned against God (v.7-11) by their unbelief and complaints (e.g., Num.11), the psalm starts with the author humbling himself and his people before God – an example we can all follow.

[1] Lord, through all the generations you have been our home! Before the mountains were born, before you gave birth to the earth and the world, from beginning to end, you are God. [3] You turn people back to dust, saying, "return to dust, you mortals!" [4] For you, a thousand years are as a passing day, as brief as a few night hours. [5] You sweep people away like dreams that disappear. They are like grass that springs up in the morning. [6] In the morning it blooms and flourishes, but by evening it is dry and withered.

As we humble ourselves it is good and right to confess where we have fallen short as Moses did.

[7] We wither beneath your anger; we are overwhelmed by your fury. [8] You spread out our sins before you— our secret sins—and you see them all. [9] We live our lives beneath your wrath, ending our years with a groan. [10] Seventy years are given to us! Some even live to eighty. But even the best years are filled with pain and trouble; soon they disappear, and we fly away. [11] Who can comprehend the power of your anger? Your wrath is as awesome as the fear you deserve. [12] Teach us to realize the brevity of life, so that we may grow in wisdom.

---

[3] Hebrew Book 4 comprises psalm 90 to 106

Having humbled ourselves and confessed our shortcomings to God, then it is good and right to praise God while asking for our daily needs. We each need to remind ourselves of God's love, *'new every morning his mercies begin (Lam.3 v.22-23)'* and remind ourselves that our hope in God is well founded (Lam.3 v.24).

> [13] O LORD, come back to us! How long will you delay? Take pity on your servants! [14] Satisfy us each morning with your unfailing love, so we may sing for joy to the end of our lives. [15] Give us gladness in proportion to our former misery! Replace the evil years with good. [16] Let us, your servants, see you work again; let our children see your glory. [17] And may the Lord our God show us his approval and make our efforts successful. Yes, make our efforts successful!

A poem based on Psalm 90: -

> *We are but grass that flourishes*
> *today and withers tomorrow*
> *Our lives are brief our toils are hard.*
> *We may live with youthful zest*
> *But collapse with bitterness when*
> *The tables are turned on us*
> *Have mercy God, give us wise hearts*
> *To seek your face, to turn to you*
> *To walk in your ways, to find your grace*
> *To give you praise and live in your love.*

A prayer: Have your way O Lord in me!

PSALM 91

¹ Those who live in the shelter of the Most High will find rest in the shadow of the Almighty. ² This I declare about the LORD: He alone is my refuge, my place of safety; he is my God, and I trust him. ³ For he will rescue you from every trap and protect you from deadly disease. ⁴ He will cover you with his feathers. He will shelter you with his wings. His faithful promises are your armour and protection. ⁵ Do not be afraid of the terrors of the night, nor the arrow that flies in the day. ⁶ Do not dread the disease that stalks in darkness, nor the disaster that strikes at midday. ⁷ Though a thousand fall at your side, though ten thousand are dying around you, these evils will not touch you. ⁸ Just open your eyes, and see how the wicked are punished.

God does not promise to deliver us from the suffering that others also endure. But God does promise to give us the strength to endure, looking only to him and not in fear of the events we are facing. So, the Psalmist's claim here would be fool-hardy if it were taken to imply that those with faith will never suffer betrayal, torture and death as Jesus himself endured, or that the faithful will never suffer disease or illness. However, we should read it as encouraging the faithful to seek to dwell in God's presence at all times through all dangers and setbacks looking only to God our Saviour as the author and provider of his grace that keeps us from being overcome by all evils that may afflict us.

⁹ If you make the LORD your refuge, if you make the Most High your shelter, ¹⁰ no evil will conquer you; no plague will come near your home. ¹¹ For he will order his angels to protect you wherever you go. ¹² They will hold you up with their hands so you won't even hurt your foot on a stone. ¹³ You will trample upon lions and cobras; you will crush fierce lions and serpents under your feet!

The NT records Satan as quoting verse eleven to the Lord Jesus Christ when he was being tested at the start of his ministry in the wilderness. The Devil had suggested he throw himself from the temple roof in Jerusalem so that God's angels would be forced to catch him in full view of the multitudes who would then flock to follow him as their Messiah.[4] Jesus repelled the temptation by quoting another scripture that we must not put God to the test (Deut.6 v.16) in order to avoid trusting totally God: instead, we are called to trust God with all our heart, mind and will. This will mean that God will turn up in response to faith, but even if he does not appear to do so, we will continue to trust God! At other times God specifically invites us to test him so as to prove the substance of our faith; for example, when challenging our commitment to give what is due to God (Malachi 3 v.10).

[14] The LORD says, "I will rescue those who love me. I will protect those who trust in my name. [15] When they call on me, I will answer; I will be with them in trouble. I will rescue and honour them. [16] I will reward them with a long life and give them my salvation."

Faith is God's mutual test that causes us to pray and give generously and see God's rule of love grow.

A poem on this theme:

God, I trust you – don't let me go!
God I will trust you; help me let go
Of all other, to depend only on You!
God, I trust you – help me follow
Help me see clearly the way to go,
Your path laid out for me - Your will to do!

A prayer: Teach me your way O lord. Amen

---

[4] By mere human thought this path might appear to fulfil God's intent for his Messiah, but would have utterly failed because it was not God's way.

Psalm 91

PSALM 92

This psalm was favoured by the Hebrews to sing for Sabbath Day celebrations emphasising as it does the call to give thanks to God morning and evening and doing so communally with song and music.

¹ It is good to give thanks to the LORD, to sing praises to the Most-High. ² It is good to proclaim your unfailing love in the morning, your faithfulness in the evening, ³ accompanied by a ten-stringed instrument, a harp, and the melody of a lyre. ⁴ You thrill me, LORD, with all you have done for me! I sing for joy because of what you have done. ⁵ O LORD, … And how deep are your thoughts.

The Psalmist is quite human thanking God for the downfall of his enemies (v.11), and finishing the psalm with a note of confident faith in the benefits of worshipping God (v.12-15).

¹² But the godly will flourish like palm trees and grow strong like the cedars of Lebanon. ¹³ For they are transplanted to the LORD's own house. They flourish in the courts of our God. ¹⁴ Even in old age they will still produce fruit; they will remain vital and green. ¹⁵ They will declare, "The LORD is just! He is my rock! There is no evil in him!"

A poem reflecting some of the theme of Psalm 92: -

Awake each morn and fill your house with praise
To God for all the blessings of your days:
Proclaim God's truth and goodness in his ways;
Join hearts in song your merry sound to raise
So, when the sunset tolls the end of day,
And western sky so warms the heart to stay
Knowing God's presence then calling you to pray
With thanksgiving and so in rest to lay.

A prayer: O Lord our God help us to put aside set times to worship and to pray.

PSALM 93

¹ The LORD is king! He is robed in majesty. Indeed, the LORD is robed in majesty and armed with strength. The world stands firm and cannot be shaken. ² Your throne, O LORD, has stood from time immemorial. You yourself are from the everlasting past. ³ The floods have risen up, O LORD. The floods have roared like thunder; the floods have lifted their pounding waves. ⁴ But mightier than the violent raging of the seas, mightier than the breakers on the shore— the LORD above is mightier than these! ⁵ Your royal laws cannot be changed. Your reign, O LORD, is holy forever and ever.

At times we may feel overwhelmed for example when faced with the loss of a loved one, or facing serious illness or unemployment, or the effects of a Corona-virus pandemic, or war, eviction from our home, etc. At such times we may echo the Psalmist sentiment that the floods around us are roaring like thunder and their pounding waves are battering us. And we can take heart from the Psalmist who reminds us that the Lord God is mightier than all that seeks to overwhelm us!

The psalmist also reminds us that God's royal laws of sacrificial love and care of others are inviable. And so, we must trust and obey in all our times of woe as well as when life is plain sailing.

A poem reflecting Psalm 93: -

God, you are above all my woes
The storm rages - please bring me through.
Even as I am overwhelmed
My heart faints, but I call to you.
Lord help me grasp your embrace
You love me, and I love you too.

A prayer: Hold me Lord so that I don't despair. Amen

PSALM 94

This psalm is a prayer and cry for justice to God the ultimate judge of all.

¹ O LORD, the God of vengeance ... let your glorious justice shine forth! ² Arise, O Judge of the earth. Give the proud what they deserve. ³ How long, O LORD? How long will the wicked be allowed to gloat? ⁴ How long will they speak with arrogance? How long will these evil people boast? ⁵ They crush your people, LORD, hurting those you claim as your own. ⁶ They kill widows and foreigners and murder orphans.

"Vengeance is mine!" says the Lord (Deut.32 v.35 & Rom.12 v.17-19)". This quotation from both the Torah and the NT (Ingil) points to the Divine requirement that humanity must not exact vengeance on people but leave justice to God, who alone judges justly. God sees people's hearts both those who believe they have been wronged as well as those who perpetrate wrong doing. We each need to look at our own short-comings before we point any fingers at others!

⁹ Is he deaf—the one who made your ears? Is he blind—the one who formed your eyes? ¹⁰ He punishes the nations—won't he also punish you? He knows everything—doesn't he also know what you are doing? ¹¹ The LORD knows people's thoughts; he knows they are worthless!

It is often those who put their trust in God who are persecuted by fanatics of another faith to theirs and sometimes their own. God sees their persecutors' hearts – God sees their pride and God will bring judgements on them if not in this life, then in the next! Those who call out to God to save them not depending on their own supposed righteousness, God lovingly supports and gives strength to endure and overcome!

¹⁴ The LORD will not reject his people; he will not abandon his special possession. ... ¹⁶ Who will protect me from the wicked? ... ¹⁷ Unless the LORD had helped me, I would soon have settled in the silence of the grave. ¹⁸ I cried out, "I am slipping!" but your unfailing love, O LORD, supported me. ¹⁹ When doubts filled my mind, your comfort gave me renewed hope and cheer.

²⁰ Can unjust leaders claim that God is on their side—leaders whose decrees permit injustice? ²¹ They gang up against the righteous and condemn the innocent to death. ²² But the LORD is my fortress; my God is the mighty rock where I hide. ²³ God will turn the sins of evil people back on them. ...

The psalm ends on a sobering note for national leaders who may be tempted to allow injustice and persecution to prevail. There are many current examples in the world where innocent people are condemned to death and where national leaders struggle with their own religious fanatics. This isn't always straight forward. For example, many minority women and girls living in the Indian sub-continent are kidnapped often forcibly converted and raped by fanatical and wicked men. Minority people are often falsely accused of blasphemy and brought before the courts to face the death sentence. Higher court judges and government ministers seeking to stand for justice in such situations have at times been murdered, condemned by hard-line religious leaders. All those who have stood up for the oppressed will nevertheless receive God's praise for their courage fighting injustice, since God is just``.

A poem based on Psalm 94: -

O God of justice, save, we pray, all those
trampled by the strong.
Give hope and strength to the poor and weak,
those despised too long.

A prayer: O lord save me from despising the weak, help me seek true justice and freedom for all to choose their way.

PSALM 95

This psalm is a call for our renewed worship of God — suitable for the start of the day or the week or a new year.

1 Come, let us sing to the Lord! Let us shout joyfully to the Rock of our salvation. 2 Let us come before him with thanksgiving. Let us sing psalms of praise to him. 3 For the Lord is great God ... 5 The sea belongs to him, for he made it. His hands formed the dry land, too. 6 Come, let us worship and bow down. Let us kneel before the Lord our maker, 7 for he is our God.

This is a great call to worship God, because God is our creator and watches over all he has made and those who call on him. The psalmist shows us that those who have found God to be 'the Rock of their salvation' have even more to celebrate than the rest of creation and should worship God with thanksgiving, with joy and singing, with praise and with humility.

7 If only you would listen to his voice today! 8 The Lord says, "Don't harden your heart as Israel did at Meribah ... 11 So in my anger I took an oath: 'They will never enter my place of rest.'"

The Hebrew psalmist refers to a time when the Hebrew slaves escaping from Egypt under the gracious deliverance of God, nevertheless moaned and complained instead of giving thanks and honour to God for their deliverance. They arrived at Meribah and found no water; subsequently God through Moses had provided them with water from a rock face.

The Psalmist perceived that ingratitude angers God as much as it does us. The Scripture tells us that when God finished his work of creation, he rested on the seventh day. And so, the Psalmist reminds us that the consequence of ingratitude is our inability to receive the promised rest that God enjoys and wants his people to share in. So (v.7), he bid his readers not to harden their hearts against God's word to them and to ever be thankful for their salvation and recommit themselves to worship and faith in all circumstances. We would do well to heed this warning!

A poem on this theme: -
Come let us worship Father God
Our saviour, ever new ever old,
Given in Christ to show the way
With gratitude we bow before him.
Whatever circumstances bring
We'll bow the knee and worship God.

A prayer: Lord God, help us to have tender and grateful hearts towards you. Amen

PSALM 96

This psalm celebrates the joy of community worship in festival seasons and the joy of all earth's eco-systems when its peoples live in righteousness and peace.

¹ Sing a new song to the Lord! Let the whole earth sing to the Lord! ² Sing to the Lord; praise his name. Each day proclaim the good news that he saves. ³ Publish his glorious deeds among the nations. Tell everyone about the amazing things he does. ⁴ Great is the Lord! He is most worthy of praise! He is to be feared above all gods. ⁵ The gods of other nations are mere idols, but the Lord made the heavens! ...

The Holy Psalms of David (Zabur)

> [7] O nations of the world, recognize the LORD; recognize that the LORD is glorious and strong. ... [11] Let the heavens be glad, and the earth rejoice! Let the sea and everything in it shout his praise! [12] Let the fields and their crops burst out with joy! Let the trees of the forest sing for joy [13] before the LORD, for he is coming! ... He will judge the world with justice, and the nations with his truth.

The Psalmist isn't merely speaking about the writing and singing of hymns and songs to God *(see end note for comment on Christian worship)*. In verse three he urges everyone to proclaim the deeds that they believe are attributable to God alone, which include their testimonies to miracles of deliverance. And in verses 5-13 he called on the nations of the world to recognise and submit to Almighty God, and in verse 11 & 12 he metaphorically called on all eco-systems to sing God's praise in recognition that God will ultimately bring justice and liberation to the earth's ecosystems as well as its peoples.

This psalm is also a call for all governments to act to ensure that the environment is properly cared for not just for the sake of their people but for God's sake, and for them not to hinder their people from knowing and worshipping the God of all creation since God is the judge of all.

A Christian poem based on this theme: -

> *Father God, your deeds are true,*
> *Shown to us in Christ, our Lord*
> *Father thank you for your gift.*
> *You have made us one with him.*
> *And one in him we live in you.*

A prayer: Father God may your love in Christ be proclaimed in all the earth and may we properly care for the world you have created. Amen!

PSALM 97

This psalm celebrates God's divine kingship.

¹ The LORD is king! Let the earth rejoice! Let the farthest coastlands be glad. ² Dark clouds surround him. Righteousness and justice are the foundation of his throne. ... ⁵ The mountains melt like wax before the LORD, before the Lord of all the earth. ⁶ The heavens proclaim his righteousness; every nation sees his glory ... ¹⁰ You who love the LORD, hate evil! He protects the lives of his godly people and rescues them from the power of the wicked. ¹¹ Light shines on the godly, and joy on those whose hearts are right ...

The ancient and highly metaphorical themes and language of this psalm should not obscure the relevance of its message in the twenty-first century. Regardless of your creed, it is a call to living rightly by all people and by the earth's eco-systems. For Christians it is a reminder that regardless of any opposition that right living may give rise to, we should always rejoice in God, since all who oppose truth, justice and mercy are opposing God and we are called to be his children (1 Pet.4 v.13).

A modern poem inspired by this ancient psalm: -
> *People of planet earth rejoice*
> *For with salvation, God's justice sings:*
> *Godly living shines forth God's light.*
> *Hate the evil that dominance brings.*
> *The earth's not ours, but to its care*
> *Take your responsibility.*
> *With all life ensure you share, so*
> *Honour the giver of earth's bounty!*

A prayer: O Spirit of God, help us honour and care for this wonderful universe and all its peoples. Amen

The Holy Psalms of David (Zabur)

PSALM 98

This psalm celebrates renewal and salvation!

¹ Sing a new song to the LORD, for he has done wonderful deeds. His right hand has won a mighty victory; his holy arm has shown his saving power! ² The LORD has announced his victory and has revealed his righteousness to every nation!

Although it is good for song-writers to compose new songs in praise of God, the real import of these verses relates to God revealing his righteousness in the current age and in the future! The original context relating to the Israelites may or may not be lost to us, but the Book of the 'Revelation of Jesus Christ' points us to their on-going and future relevance. For in Rev.21 we read,

"³Look, God's home is among his people! He will live with them, and they will be his people!" ... ⁵And the one sitting on the throne said, "Look, I am making everything new! ... ⁶It is finished, I am the Beginning and the End! To all who are thirsty I will freely give of the water of life. ⁷All who are victorious will inherit all these blessings, and I will be their God and they shall be my people"... ⁹Then one of the seven angels ... said to me, "Come with me! I will show you the bride, the wife of the Lamb." ¹⁰ So he took me in the Spirit to a great, high mountain, and he showed me the holy city, Jerusalem, descending out of heaven from God. ¹¹ It shone with the glory of God and sparkled like a precious stone—like jasper as clear as crystal. ¹² The city wall was broad and high, with twelve gates guarded by twelve angels. And the <u>names of the twelve tribes of Israel were written on the gates</u>.¹³ There were three gates on each side—east, north, south, and west. ¹⁴ The wall of the <u>city had twelve foundation stones, and on them were written the names of the twelve apostles of the Lamb</u>.

I have underlined two particular phrases that together point to both the faithful people of Israel and to the faithful Christian church of Jesus Christ as constituting the 'Bride of the Lamb of God, i.e., the Bride of Christ. Also, we can see from the Gospels of Jesus that Jesus spoke of the 'House (i.e., 'faithful') of Israel (Matt.15 v.24)' and of the disciples being 'given authority over the twelve tribes of Israel (Matt.19 v.28).' What is happening here? It is clear that the Bible NT (Ingil) regards God's glory (i.e., God's 'righteousness') being revealed to all nations by means of Christ's church and by a new faithful Israel. The 'house'/ faithful of Israel are not replaced by the 'house'/ faithful of Christ's Church! Nor should Muslims think the faithful of Christ's church and the faithful of the Jews are ever replaced by the faithful of Islam (as Surah 5:69 warns)! There is only one God and only one Lamb of God, Jesus the Christ, who has authority over his Church and over the 'house' of Israel, and wherever there are Muslims who receive the Lamb of God (ref. Rev.21 v.26), then I would venture there will be a 'house' of Islam (i.e., those coming to faith from an Islamic background) as there is a house of Israel and Christ's church in God's coming kingdom!

The Psalm goes on speak of God's coming judgement on all nations of the planet.

> ... **⁴ Shout to the LORD, all the earth; break out in praise and sing for joy! ⁵ Sing your praise to the LORD with the harp, with the harp and melodious song, ⁶ with trumpets and the sound of the ram's horn. Make a joyful symphony before the LORD, the King! ⁷ Let the sea and everything in it shout his praise! Let the earth and all living things join in. ⁸ Let the rivers clap their hands in glee! Let the hills sing out their songs of joy ⁹ before the LORD, for he is coming to judge the earth. He will judge the world with justice, and the nations with fairness.**

God will judge the peoples of earth by their hearts' response to his word become flesh (John 1 v.4-13).

Psalm 98

We must not shout God's praise with protestations of our own righteousness but instead with joyful wonder at all creation and the inner strength of God's Spirit in us, displayed in living unselfishly and facing off all evil: and then our songs will be an encouragement to all of God's creatures!

A poem inspired by Psalm 98: -

>*Lord help me wonder at all you are;*
>
>*Ponder all you do and all you give.*
>
>*Spirit of God steer my hand to care,*
>
>*To serve and for others there to be,*
>
>*Then will all my praise to God ring true*
>
>*Both on earth and in eternity!*

A prayer: - Lord we love you. Amen

PSALM 99

This psalm calls us to worship God our eternal king!

¹ The LORD is king! Let the nations tremble! He sits on his throne between the cherubim. Let the whole earth quake! ² The LORD sits in majesty in Jerusalem, exalted above all the nations. ³ Let them praise your great and awesome name. Your name is holy! ⁴ Mighty King, lover of justice, you have established fairness. You have acted with justice and righteousness throughout Israel. ⁵ Exalt the LORD our God! Bow low before his feet, for he is holy!

The Psalmist reference in verse 1, is to the symbolic throne of God wrought in gold on the lid of the covenant box containing the stone tablets given to Moses on Mount Sinai. The tablets were the first written commandments from God (later spelt out in the Ten Commandments given to Israel). This symbolic throne was called God's Mercy Seat and it sat between two cherubim also wrought in gold on the lid of the box. It was the central and most holy item in the Hebrew sanctuary. It was kept in the 'Most Holy of holies' and was where the high priest went on behalf of the people of Israel to make the annual sacrifice for the forgiveness of his own and the people's sins. This covenant box came to be kept in Jerusalem; hence, the Psalmist writes that the Holy God of Creation is exalted above all nations from Jerusalem and calls on the nations of the world (v.3) to praise and worship God who acts with justice, righteousness and with mercy. We can also note that from this symbolism, that Almighty God's character is revealed as based on truth, righteousness, justice and mercy.

⁶ Moses and Aaron were among his priests; Samuel also called on his name. They cried to the LORD for help, and he answered them. ⁷ He spoke to Israel from the pillar of cloud, and they followed the laws and decrees he gave them. ⁸ O LORD our God, you answered them. You were a forgiving God to them, but you punished them when they went wrong. ⁹ Exalt the LORD our God, and worship at his holy mountain in Jerusalem, for the LORD our God is holy!

The Psalmist concludes with some examples of those who had faith in this revelation of Almighty God and adds the warning that God also punishes his faithful when they stray in order to help them turn back to faith.

Poem for Psalm 99 on this theme: -

> *Lord you are Great in goodness*
> *You are great in justice,*
> *In truth, in love and mercy:*
> *God help me keep faith in you,*
> *So, with your help each day,*
> *For others live in your way!*

Prayer: Amen!

PSALM 100

This psalm calls on God's people to enter God's 'gates' with thanksgiving and praise!

¹ Shout with joy to the LORD, all the earth! ² Worship the LORD with gladness. Come before him, singing with joy. ³ Acknowledge that the LORD is God! He made us, and we are his. We are his people, the sheep of his pasture. ⁴ Enter his gates with thanksgiving; go into his courts with praise. Give thanks to him and praise his name. ⁵ For the LORD is good. His unfailing love continues forever, and his faithfulness continues to each generation.

How great is the creator God of the universe! And when we acknowledge that God is our Lord and that we are his people, our joy should be exuberant!

The Psalmist here points us to how we should enter God's holy presence – not by our outward prostrations or appearances, but with our heartfelt gratitude for God's mercy and goodness to us. As Jesus commented to Simon the Pharisee (Lk.7 v.47), 'Who do you think loves God the most, one who knows he/she have been forgiven much or one who has been forgiven little?' The implication was that Simon loved God little because he was proud of his own supposed righteousness.

Andrew Jones has pointed out the Psalms 94 to 107 are 'community psalms' and though we may relate them to ourselves as individuals, we also need to read and pray them as community prayers and worship. Here there is strength and joy in singing God's praises together with like-minded people.

A poem on this theme: -
  O Creator God, we are your people
  You have shown us your kingdom of love.
  You love us with an everlasting love:
  You have made us your people of praise!
  You have called and sealed us with your Spirit;
  You have put your word into our hearts!
  We will serve you with thanksgiving and love!
  We will take your name to all the earth!

A prayer: Lord may we reflect the glory of your people.

PSALM 101

The psalm divides into the king's inward heart attitude (v.1-3a) and then his outward heart intention in relation to other people (v.3b-8) and is a beautiful example of the heart attitudes religious communities and their leaderships should exemplify in every age.

> ¹**I will sing of your love and justice, LORD. I will praise you with songs. ²I will be careful to live a blameless life—when will you come to help me? I will lead a life of integrity in my own home. ³I will refuse to look at anything vile and vulgar.**

These are challenging personal precepts for today with our multimedia choices available within our own homes.

> **I hate all who deal crookedly; I will have nothing to do with them. ⁴I will reject perverse ideas and stay away from every evil. ⁵I will not tolerate people who slander their neighbours. I will not endure conceit and pride. ⁶I will search for faithful people to be my companions. Only those who are above reproach will be allowed to serve me.**

⁷I will not allow deceivers to serve in my house, and liars will not stay in my presence. ⁸My daily task will be to ferret out the wicked and free the city of the LORD from their grip.

These personal action precepts are as valid today as ever and particularly for leaders who are under constant media scrutiny. However, Verse 7 should not be read as a charter for religious extremists. It is a reference to all those who deliberately create fake news and deliberately falsify the truth: this does not relate to anyone who sincerely believes a particular religious creed or hold to a particular doctrine.

Poem drawn from this psalm: -
Teach me your ways O Lord
That I may be blameless on judgement day.
And help me not to envy
The wicked in their vulgar thought and way.

Prayer: Lord help me lead a life of integrity in my own home.

PSALM 102

This penitential psalm is set out as a lament and appears to be written by an author who is either depressed or chronically sick. In the middle the author may have inserted a song which is appropriate to help lift the mood. The author reflects on the Lord's timelessness compared to our brevity and concludes that though we wither and die like grass at least God will continue to watch over and bless our future generations - those who call on the Lord in their time. Hence the importance of recording our testimony for the sake of our descendants.

¹LORD, hear my prayer! Listen to my plea! ²Don't turn away from me in my time of distress. ... ³For my days disappear like smoke, ... ⁴My heart is sick, withered like grass, and I have lost my appetite. ...

⁶ I am like an owl in the desert, like a little owl in a far-off wilderness. ...¹¹ My life passes as swiftly as the evening shadows. I am withering away like grass.

¹² But you, O LORD, will sit on your throne forever. Your fame will endure to every generation. ³ You will arise and have mercy on Jerusalem— and now is the time to pity her, now is the time you promised to help. ¹⁴ For your people love every stone in her walls and cherish even the dust in her streets. ¹⁵ Then the nations will tremble before the LORD. ... ¹⁶ For the LORD will rebuild Jerusalem. He will appear in his glory. ¹⁷ He will listen to the prayers of the destitute. He will not reject their pleas. ¹⁸ Let this be recorded for future generations, so that a people not yet born will praise the LORD. ...

These verses speak of a rebuilding of Jerusalem (which has been rebuilt several times in history), but also metaphorically of a time when God will 'appear in his glory (v.16)' to build the spiritual' Jerusalem, i.e., the city of God *(Rev.21, ref. also Psalm 122 hereunder).*

²⁵ Long ago you laid the foundation of the earth and made the heavens with your hands. ²⁶ They will perish, but you remain forever; they will wear out like old clothing. You will change them like a garment and discard them. ²⁷ But you are always the same; you will live forever. ²⁸ The children of your people will live in security. Their children's children will thrive in your presence.

The psalmist goes on to speak of God wrapping up this physical universe and replacing it with a new eternal existence where God's children will live in God's presence. In the same way the NT speaks (1 Cor. 15 v.35-58) of those whom God redeems (from these mortal bodies) being provided with new 'heavenly' bodies to live in eternity with God.

A poem on this theme: -
O God when I am sick or depressed,
Help me to recall all your faithfulness
And pass on to the next generation
My testimony to all your goodness!
Our hope is for your glory, your righteousness
Forever infused into your people
Now thankfully living in eternity
Blessed forever with all God's faithful.

A prayer: Thank you Lord God your faithfulness endures to all generations! Amen

PSALM 103

This psalm celebrates God's eternal love for us!

¹Let all that I am praise the Lord; with my whole heart, I will praise his holy name. ... ³He forgives all my sins and heals all my diseases. ⁴He redeems me from death and crowns me with love and tender mercies.

The Psalmist is full of joy and is wholeheartedly dedicated to God and the cause of praising God for all he is. The prophet King David shows us that the truth of the forgiveness of sins needs to be proclaimed worldwide. There are millions who strive by pious acts, by self-sacrifice, by prayers, by martyrdom to seek the forgiveness of their sins - but all will be to no avail.

Jesus (the Christ) was the only sinless prophet and one Christ in whom God fully dwelt (2 Cor. 5 v.13) so that in him God forgives the sins of all who turn away from themselves and turn to God in faith. Yes, God's purpose is to redeem people from spiritual death - And he does that through the forgiveness of sins and giving his Spirit to enable people to magnify his name!

> **⁷He revealed his character to Moses ... ⁸The Lord is compassionate and merciful, slow to anger and filled with unfailing love...**

The truth is that God is compassionate and merciful and he doesn't treat us as our sins deserve. For he knows our weakness. God calls everyone he has made to be like him in character, to be compassionate and merciful to everyone else. There is no callousness or cruelty or self-centred pride in God's dealings with us! For God wants all people to come into close relationship with himself and with all other people. It is the sin of our self-centred pride, our cruelty and callousness to others that keeps God away from us and us from God. As the Book of God shows us, no self-sacrifice, no pious duty, no pilgrimage, no act of charity, no martyrdom will absolve us from our sin unless we repent and turn our hearts and ways over to God's compassion and mercy shown in Christ.

The Muslim Holy Koran repeats the same message of Allah's compassion and mercy in its opening Surah. Any other revelation or sayings of a prophet that contradicts this revealed character of God is to be rejected - it is of human origin, not of God's Spirit. And as the Gospel of Jesus tells us it is only by God's grace through faith in God's Christ that we can receive His Spirit to enable us to emulate God's character.

> **¹¹For his unfailing love towards those who hear him is as great as the height of the heavens above the earth. ¹²He has removed our sins as far as the east is from the west. ¹³The Lord is like a (good) father to his children, tender and compassionate to those who fear him. ²¹. praise the Lord you armies of angels who serve him and do his will! ... ²². Let all that I am praise the Lord.**

The book of God tells us *'If I could speak all the languages of earth and of angels (or if I gave everything I have to the poor and even sacrificed my body), but I didn't love others, I would a noisy gong. I would have gained nothing.'* God is father-like to all who fear (respect and love) him.

Psalm 103

Let us do that and let us praise God for his compassion and mercy with our lips and with our lives. Amen!

A poem from Psalm 103: -

There is no good deed, no self-sacrifice,
Enough to earn your love, Lord God:
Only one: - Your grace offered out to all
Who receive your free gift in Christ!

A prayer: I turn myself over to you my God, forgive my sin through your love in Christ Jesus. Amen

PSALM 104

A psalm celebrating Creator God!

¹ Let all that I am praise the LORD. O LORD my God, how great you are! You are robed with honour and majesty. ² You are dressed in a robe of light. ... ⁴ The winds are your messengers; flames of fire are your servants ('He sends his angels like winds and his servants like flames of fire' Gk[5]).

When we gratefully appreciate the wonders of the universe and the planet God has given us, we will appreciate the privilege to share in God's care for all creation. The Septuagint translators (v.4) recognised that God is still intimately at work in the universe calling us to faith and responsible living.

⁵ You placed the world on its foundation so it would never be moved. ⁶ You clothed the earth with floods of water ... ⁸ Mountains rose and valleys sank to the levels you decreed. ⁹ Then you set a firm boundary for the seas, so they would never again cover the earth.

---

[5] Gk. i.e. the Septuagint translation from Hebrew to Greek in 300 BCE

In verses 6 to 9 the Psalmist is clearly referring to the early chapters of the book of Genesis that metaphorically describe the formation of the planet and the great flood at the time of Noah. The point the Psalmist makes is that God is ultimately responsible for our planet and our security, even though we have been appointed as its stewards. This includes the provision of fertile soils, forests, seas, weathering, minerals, natural erosion, tsunamis and natural climate change in a process that took place over a vast time scale compared to that of a single human generation. Genesis also speaks of God creating our species to help care for the earth and its ecosystems, plants and animals. When humanity destroys fertile land by de-forestation, accelerates climate change by burning too much fossil fuel, destroys major ecosystems such as rain forests and coral reefs and drives many other species to extinction, we fail to act responsibly as God intends us to do.

10 You make springs pour water into the ravines, so streams gush down from the mountains. 11 They provide water for all the animals, and the wild donkeys quench their thirst. 12 The birds nest beside the streams and sing among the branches of the trees. 13 You send rain on the mountains from your heavenly home, and you fill the earth with the fruit of your labour. 14 You cause grass to grow for the livestock and plants for people to use. You allow them to produce food from the earth— 15 wine to make them glad, olive oil to soothe their skin, and bread to give them strength. 16 The trees of the LORD are well cared for— the cedars of Lebanon that he planted. 17 There the birds make their nests, and the storks make their homes in the cypresses. 18 High in the mountains live the wild goats, and the rocks form a refuge for the hyraxes (dassies).

This wonderful hymn of praise covers the bountiful provision all creatures are meant to enjoy (whether that be birds, plants, animals or ourselves).

And verse 14 says that God graciously 'allows' humanity to cultivate the planet responsibly and provide ourselves with good things as part of this provision.

> [19] **You made the moon to mark the seasons, and the sun knows when to set. [20] You send the darkness, and it becomes night, when all the forest animals prowl about. [21] Then the young lions roar for their prey, stalking the food provided by God. [22] At dawn they slink back into their dens to rest. [23] Then people go off to their work, where they labour until evening. [24] O LORD, what a variety of things you have made! In wisdom you have made them all! The earth is full of your creatures. [25] Here is the ocean, vast and wide, teeming with life of every kind ... [27] They all depend on you to give them food as they need it. ... When you take away their breath, they die and turn again to dust. [30] When you give them your breath (or send your Spirit), life is created, and you renew the face of the earth. ...**

Advances in science have shown the evidence for all species having evolved from earlier living organisms however that evolution may have happened. And it is clear that successful adaptation to environmental change or extinction, has been a major driver: however, the precise mechanism for the genetic improvements involved, is not currently understood. People of faith can know categorically that God by his Spirit is intimately involved in the generation of all life (ref. v.30).

> **The LORD takes pleasure in all he has made! ... [33] I will sing to the LORD as long as I live. I will praise my God to my last breath! [34] May all my thoughts be pleasing to him, for I rejoice in the LORD. ... Let all that I am praise the LORD!**

A poem from Psalm 104

I will sing your praise all my days!
In wisdom you have made all things!
You call us to take care of all
That swims, or walks or flies with wings.
Life's ecosystems are all linked:
With good care your creation sings!
O lord our God how great you are -
Your life in us true wholeness brings!

A prayer: May your life be manifest in me. Amen

PSALM 105

A psalm celebrating God's covenant relationship with his people!

¹ **Give thanks to the LORD and proclaim his greatness. Let the whole world know what he has done.** ² **Sing to him; yes, sing his praises. Tell everyone about his wonderful deeds.** ³ **Exult in his holy name; rejoice, you who worship the LORD.**

⁴ **Search for the LORD and for his strength; continually seek him.** ⁵ **Remember the wonders he has performed, his miracles, and the rulings he has given,** ⁶ **you children of his servant Abraham, ... his chosen ones.** ⁷ **He is the LORD our God. His justice is seen throughout the land.** ⁸ **He always stands by his covenant - the commitment he made to a thousand generations.**

The children of God's servant Abraham being addressed by this psalm are not necessarily the Israelites, but rather, all those throughout the world who exercise faith in the living creator God as the NT reminds us. John the Baptist in calling the Jews to repentance declared, 'God can raise up children of Abraham from the very stones of the river bed (Matt. 3 v.9).'

And NT prophet St. Paul declared that Abraham's children are all those who have the same kind of faith in God that Abraham displayed (Gal.3 v.6,7).

> **14 Yet he did not let anyone oppress them. He warned kings on their behalf: 15 "Do not touch my chosen people, and do not hurt my prophets." 16 He called for a famine on the land of Canaan, cutting off its food supply. 17 Then he sent someone to Egypt ahead of them - Joseph, who was sold as a slave. 18 They bruised his feet with fetters and placed his neck in an iron collar. 19 Until the time came to fulfil his dreams, the LORD tested Joseph's character. 20 Then Pharaoh sent for him and set him free; the ruler of the nation opened his prison door.**

The psalmist goes on to tell the story of the children of Israel being delivered from slavery in Egypt by God under the hand of Moses. This should remind all people of faith of the importance of telling our stories and our testimonies of God's deliverance. It is too easy to let God's faithfulness in our generation slip into oblivion without it being passed on to succeeding generations in faith. Today we have far greater media opportunity than ever before and we should carefully provide succeeding generations with testimonies of God's dealings with us and all people of faith throughout the world. The covenant (promise) God made with Abraham was that by his faith, God would bless the whole world.

A poem around this psalm:

> *The past generations*
> *Of your glory did speak*
> *O Lord God, our Father,*
> *By faith we can too!*
> *You were faithful to them;*
> *You are faithful to us:*
> *Their faith moved the mountains,*
> *Our faith will do too!*

Great is your faithfulness
We will tell of it, so,
The next generation
Will follow you too!

A prayer: Dear Father God, help us connect each generation with you. Amen

PSALM 106

The psalm laments the community's unfaithfulness to their saviour God. The Psalmist opens and ends with a paean of praise (v.1-3 & v.48) despite being in exile in a foreign land! He then moves into personal prayer (v.4-5) and a general confession (v.6) before meditating on God's past dealings with his people in bringing them out of slavery in Egypt (v.7-46). He describes their fickleness in thanking God for deliverance and yet soon forgetting all about their Saviour God. And yet God persisted with them rescuing them when they turned back in prayer. The Psalmist concludes by reminding God of his past faithfulness and asking God to rescue his people again from exile (v.47).

¹Praise the LORD! Give thanks to the LORD, for he is good! His faithful love endures forever. ² Who can list the glorious miracles of the LORD? Who can ever praise him enough? ³ There is joy for those who deal justly with others and always do what is right.

It takes faith to praise and thank God in hard times even when you know that you may have contributed to those hard times! For we always need to be praising God who loves us with everlasting love despite our frailty and shortcomings.

⁶ Like our ancestors, we have sinned. We have done wrong! We have acted wickedly! ⁷ Our ancestors in Egypt were not impressed by the LORD's miraculous deeds. They soon forgot his many acts of kindness to them ...

[8] Even so, he saved them—to defend the honour of his name ... [10] So he rescued them from their enemies ... [12] Then his people believed his promises. Then they sang his praise. [13] Yet how quickly they forgot what he had done! They wouldn't wait for his counsel! ... testing God's patience in that dry wasteland.

[44] Even so, he pitied them in their distress and listened to their cries. [45] He remembered his covenant with them and relented because of his unfailing love. [46] He even caused their captors to treat them with kindness. [47] Save us, O LORD our God! Gather us back from among the nations, so we can thank your holy name and rejoice and praise you. [48] Praise the LORD, the God of Israel, who lives from everlasting to everlasting! Let all the people say, "Amen!" Praise the LORD!

The Psalmist described in great detail all the many sins committed by the people of Israel not only throughout their journey from captivity but also once they had settled into the land of Canaan, and how they suffered God's corrective judgement (v.6-43) and how God still persisted in calling them back to his loving kingship. And yet God had pity on them.

He does not treat us as our sins deserve! We need to learn from this to take time to remember all the way God has led us and thank God for all his mercies to us. So that we continue to thankfully follow him with true humility and faith.

A Poem based on Psalm 106: -

I will praise You God as long as I live!
Help me do so in hard times and in plenty.
Keep me praising when the going's tough
Keep me thanking through ease and rough.

A prayer: Thank you God for your love un-ending! Amen

PSALM 107

A psalm calling the community to proclaim the good things God has done for them.

¹Give thanks to the LORD, for he is good! His faithful love endures forever. ² Has the LORD redeemed you? Then speak out! Tell others he has redeemed you from your enemies. ³ For he has gathered the exiles from many lands, from east and west, from north and south. ⁴ Some wandered in the wilderness, lost and homeless. ⁵ Hungry and thirsty, they nearly died. ⁶ "LORD, help!" they cried in their trouble, and he rescued them from their distress. ⁷ He led them straight to safety, to a city where they could live. ⁸ Let them praise the LORD for his great love and for the wonderful things he has done for them. ⁹ For he satisfies the thirsty and fills the hungry with good things.

²¹ Let them praise the LORD for his great love and for the wonderful things he has done for them. ²² Let them offer sacrifices of thanksgiving and sing joyfully about his glorious acts.

The psalmist recounts many different ways people have suffered either through the vagaries and risks of life, their deliberate disobedience or by their foolish choices (v.4 to 32) and recounts how when they called out to God to save them, God responded in setting them free and/or providing for their needs. And the psalmist calls on all who have been so saved in their distress to praise God and show their thankfulness.

³³ He changes rivers into deserts, and springs of water into dry, thirsty land. ³⁴ He turns the fruitful land into salty wastelands, because of the wickedness of those who live there.

35 But he also turns deserts into pools of water, the dry land into springs of water. **36** He brings the hungry to settle there and to build their cities. **37** They sow their fields, plant their vineyards, and harvest their bumper crops. **38** How he blesses them! They raise large families there, and their herds of livestock increase. **42** The godly will see these things and be glad, while the wicked are struck silent. **43** Those who are wise will take all this to heart; they will see in our history the faithful love of the LORD.

In this second half of the psalm the psalmist speaks of God's judgements and mercies. And it is true to life that humanity has regularly sown the seeds of environmental damage causing land erosion, loss of natural habitat and species diversity, climate change and many of our ailments (v.33 – 34).

Whereas it has been the testimony of others that when they have acted on their faith in God, they have often found prosperity, but more importantly the grace to live well despite the hardships that surround them (v.35-38).

The psalmist concluded with a salutary comment (v.42-43) that reinforced his bid to the community to 'speak out the deeds of God (v.2). We also need to respond to this wise advice.

A poem based on this psalm: -

Live out your faith in God
See him turn the rocks into
Good water pools for you!
Let others know it is
God's grace at work in you
That keeps you standing tall!

A prayer: Lord may my life and words proclaim your grace at work in me. Amen

PSALM 108

This short psalm of David is full of confidence in God. The nation of Israel at the time was facing ongoing tension and war with the Edomites which wasn't going well. Nevertheless, the king's confidence was in God. He commenced his prayer with praise to God (v.1-5) and then reminds God of the promises made for his nation in the Scripture (v.8-9), before pleading for help against his enemy (v.10-13).

¹My heart is confident in you, O God; no wonder I can sing your praises with all my heart! ²Wake up, lyre and harp! I will wake the dawn with my song. ³I will thank you, LORD, among all the people. I will sing your praises among the nations. ⁴For your unfailing love is higher than the heavens. Your faithfulness reaches to the clouds. ⁵Be exalted, O God, above the highest heavens. May your glory shine over all the earth.

We too should remember it is always right and good to focus all our prayers in the context of praise to God based on our confidence in God's mercy and love for all people. A strong confidence in God is essential to our achieving any good thing in God's grace.

A poem based on Psalm 108: -

O God, my faith and trust is in you!
I am listening for your call;
Help me to quell all fears that may come
Then I know that I will stand tall!

A prayer: Help me hear and respond to you, my God. Amen

PSALM 109

The psalmist (probably King David in exile) takes his anguish over betrayal by his former friends (now enemies) to God, pleading that God restore him in their sight.

¹ O God, whom I praise, don't stand silent and aloof ² while the wicked slander me and tell lies about me. ³ They surround me with hateful words and fight against me for no reason. ⁴ I love them, but they try to destroy me with accusations even as I am praying for them! ⁵ They repay evil for good, and hatred for my love. ⁶ They say, "Get an evil person to turn against him. Send an accuser to bring him to trial. ⁷ When his case comes up for judgment, let him be pronounced guilty. Count his prayers as sins. ⁸ Let his years be few; let someone else take his position. ⁹ May his children become fatherless, and his wife a widow. ¹⁰ May his children wander as beggars ...

The psalmist felt he was hated without cause by those he had been kind to. People allow such hatred to grow in their hearts from envy of another's success, or position or their reputation or merely because others make them feel inferior. Jesus Christ was and often still is hated for the same reasons and his followers may get similar treatment. Religious persecution flows from hatred of a different culture or belief system. Sadly, people of minority cultures often face false accusations and are badly discriminated against by those in the majority culture – this is particularly so in countries governed on theocratic lines.

²⁰ May those curses become the LORD's punishment for my accusers who speak evil of me. ²¹ But deal well with me, O Sovereign LORD, for the sake of your own reputation!

Rescue me because you are so faithful and good. ²² For I am poor and needy, and my heart is full of pain. ²³ I am fading like a shadow at dusk; I am brushed off like a locust. ²⁴ My knees are weak from fasting, and I am skin and bones. ²⁵ I am a joke to people everywhere; when they see me, they shake their heads in scorn. ... ²⁶ Help me, O LORD my God! Save me because of your unfailing love. ²⁷ Let them see that this is your doing, that you yourself have done it, LORD.

David pleaded for God to save him and restore him so that his enemies couldn't fail to see that God had vindicated him.

²⁸ Then let them curse me if they like, but you will bless me! ... ²⁹ May my accusers be clothed with disgrace; may their humiliation cover them like a cloak. ³⁰ But I will give repeated thanks to the LORD, praising him to everyone. ³¹ For he stands beside the needy, ready to save them from those who condemn them.

David's faith in God held firm despite persecutions: we too need to stand firm, remembering that Christ suffered out of love for the world and calls us to love those who may persecute us and stand on his side.

A poem from Psalm 109: -

God, I hate being victimised:
Yet, you stood firm when falsely accused,
When Jesus they crucified.
God, I don't know if I would stand
But I know you can give me strength,
And help me to forgive.

A prayer: God help me not to shrink from your calling. Amen

PSALM 110

¹ The LORD said to my lord[6], "Sit in the place of honour at my right hand until I humble your enemies, making them a footstool under your feet."

² The LORD will extend your powerful kingdom from Jerusalem; you will rule over your enemies. ³ When you go to war, your people will serve you willingly. You are arrayed in holy garments, and your strength will be renewed each day like the morning dew.

⁴ The LORD has taken an oath and will not break his vow: You are a priest forever in the order of Melchizedek." ⁵ The Lord stands at your right hand to protect you. ... He will be victorious.

This psalm (in similar vein to Psalm 2) was probably written by an admirer of King David and prophetically points to God's Messiah (inspired by God's Spirit). Verse 1 can be rightly translated as 'Yahweh (Almighty God) said to my 'lord and master,' "sit at my right hand" That is to say God was giving David authority over his enemies. By the first century BCE (at the latest), this psalm was understood by the Jews as prophetic of the coming Messiah, i.e., they believed it referred to God commissioning his Messiah to bring the nations into God's kingdom. And the Jewish leaders understood by this that their Messiah would conquer the world by force.

In verse 4 the psalmist compared King David with the pre-Hebrew king called Melchizedek who had centuries before ruled Jerusalem (when it was Salem) and to whom Abram had given a tithe of the spoils of war (Genesis 14 v.17-20). The psalmist used this to illustrate his belief that David would be a priestly king like Melchizedek had been and would be God's agent in defeating

---

[6] The word translated as Lord here is not the same word as used to denote deity

Israel's enemies and bringing them to faith in God. The NT (Ingil) quotes this as prophetic of the coming of Christ Jesus God's special Messiah for the world *(see end note).*

Jesus himself quoted this psalm when confronting the Jewish religious authorities. Matt. 22 v.41-45, as follows:

> **[41]Then surrounded by Pharisees, Jesus asked them this question: "[42]What do you think about the Messiah – whose son is he?" They replied, "He is the son of David." [43]Jesus responded, "Then why does David, speaking under the inspiration of the Spirit, call the Messiah 'my Lord'? For David said, 'The Lord (God) said to my Lord (Messiah), sit in the place of honour at my right hand until I humble your enemies beneath your feet (Ps 110v1).' [45]Since David called the Messiah 'my Lord' how can the Messiah be his son?"**

Here Jesus faced the leaders with the niceties of the prophetic: they held that Psalm 110 was written by King David and that it was a God-given prophecy about the rule of the coming Messiah. They also believed that the Messiah would be a direct descendant of David and would establish Israel as the leading world nation by means of military victories (as Psalm 110 goes on to describe). Such a warrior would have showed that he was not merely David's biological descendant but would be the mightiest warrior that the Jews ever had.

Jesus was effectively challenging the orthodox view about what kind of Messiah God was going to send them. Jesus pointed out that king David's prophecy (as they believed it literally to be) implied that the Messiah is of a status quite unlike that of a descendant of David or even that of a mighty warrior in battle. For David to call him 'lord and master', a term that could be used to address a highly exalted earthly ruler or even God, put the Messiah above being an equal to David. It was challenges like this that eventually led the Jewish authorities to condemn Jesus to death for blasphemy.

Psalm 110

We need to think about our faith and the challenges that others make, so that we are always ready, as St. Peter bids us, 'to give a sound reason for our faith (1 Pet.3v15).'

A poem from Psalm 110

> *David's greater son, Jesus*
> *Proclaimed a priestly king by God*
> *Sits at God's right hand on high*
> *Bringing in God's kingdom rule.*

A prayer: Thank you God that part of your reality is now seen in Jesus Christ.

PSALM 111

Psalm 111 and 112 are both acrostic poems in ten stanzas. In the same spirit, I have sought to summarise each psalm in ten short numbered precepts.

¹Praise the LORD! I will thank the LORD with all my heart as I meet with his godly people. ² How amazing are the deeds of the LORD! All who delight in him should ponder them. ³ Everything he does reveals his glory and majesty. His righteousness never fails. ⁴ He causes us to remember his wonderful works. How gracious and merciful is our LORD! ⋯ ⁹ He has paid a full ransom for his people. He has guaranteed his covenant with them forever. What a holy, awe-inspiring name he has! ¹⁰ Fear of the LORD is the foundation of true wisdom. All who obey his commandments will grow in wisdom. Praise him forever!

Verse 9 particularly resonates for Christians as it themes with the prophet Isaiah's prophetic writing in Isaiah chapters 50 to 54 *(see end notes for further exposition of this).*

In lieu of a poem I offer you Ten Precepts for Christians drawn from Psalm 111: -

1) Out of your gratitude to God meet with God's people.
2) Then, together meditate on God's deeds;
3) Consider the sheer wonder of God's majesty and righteousness!
4) Give testimony to God's grace and mercy to you.
5) Remember God is faithful to his promises and feeds all hungry hearts.
6) Expect God to give you favour in the eyes of the world!
7) Know you can trust God's precepts since God is both just and good.
8) With good conscience be careful to follow in God's way for us
9) Hold firmly to the fact that God has redeemed you fully in Christ.
10) Live out your life with reverent praise, following where ever God's Spirit leads you!

A prayer: Lord help me follow these precepts in good conscience. Amen.

PSALM 112

As for the previous psalm, I summarise this psalm in ten short precepts.

¹Praise the LORD! How joyful are those who fear the LORD and delight in obeying his commands. ² Their children will be successful everywhere; an entire generation of godly people will be blessed. ...

⁶ Such people will not be overcome by evil. Those who are righteous will be long remembered. ⁷ They do not fear bad news; they confidently trust the LORD to care for them. ⁸ They are confident and fearless and can face their foes triumphantly. ...

Remember these ten precepts of Psalm 112: -

1) Be joyful as you delight in following the Lord God!
2) Your family in their generation will then be blessed.
3) Your good deeds will count for succeeding generations.
4) You will shine out God's compassion, generosity and goodness:
5) You will be blessed if you lend to others and are fair in all your dealings!
6) If you resist evil you will be remembered long after you moved on!
7) You will trust God to help you turn around bad situations:
8) You will be resilient in the face of your enemies
9) As you are generous to the poor and needy you will be held in honour!
10) Your enemies will be forced to admit that God is with you!

A prayer: Lord help me to be such a person as portrayed in this psalm. Amen

PSALM 113

This psalm properly exalts the Creator God and then focuses on God's care for the poor and lowly.

>¹Praise the LORD! Yes, give praise, O servants of the LORD. Praise the name of the LORD! … ³ Everywhere— from east to west— praise the name of the LORD. ⁴ For the LORD is high above the nations; his glory is higher than the heavens.
>⁵ Who can be compared with the LORD our God, who is enthroned on high?
>⁶ He stoops to look down on heaven and on earth. ⁷ He lifts the poor from the dust and the needy from the garbage dump. ⁸ He sets them among princes, even the princes of his own people! ⁹ He gives the childless woman a family, making her a happy mother. Praise the LORD!

There are precious promises here for those who would claim them by faith with God. However, faith always means trusting God fully and learning what his way for us will be, even if it means our dreams are not fulfilled in the way we want.

Poem drawn from Psalm 113: -

>*Dear God, unimaginably vast as the heavens, so is your glory;*
>*Yet your care reaches everyone everywhere down to each proton and quark!*
>*Your glory is seen in giving free-will to animate life, as that life*
>*Owns intimate relationship with you to bring your light into the dark!*

Prayer; How amazing God, you are closer than my very breath!

PSALM 114

¹When the Israelites escaped from Egypt— ... ²the land of Judah became God's sanctuary ... ³The Red Sea saw them coming ... ⁵What's wrong, Red Sea, that made you hurry out of their way? What happened, Jordan River, that you turned away? ⁶Why, mountains, did you skip like rams? Why, hills, like lambs? ⁷Tremble, O earth, at the presence of the Lord, at the presence of the God of Jacob. ⁸He turned the rock into a pool of water; yes, a spring of water flowed from solid rock.

What a pean of praise this psalm is! And it is the testimony of many a believer that in response to their faith, God turns their rocks and hard places into pools of life-giving water accomplishing God's way on Earth. The psalmist imagines the very elements opposing the escape of the Children of Israel from slavery in Egypt, hastily skipping out of their way when they sense the presence of their Creator God. Exercise your faith, as you walk with God this day!

Poem drawn from Psalm 114

Lord God, may your gentle presence come
As we submit to own your way:
Given freedom yet still obeying,
All creation will own your sway,
Your good laws of love compelling
Silent adoration in our day!

A prayer: Good Lord, let me own your way. Amen

PSALM 115

¹Not to us, O Lord, not to us, but to your name goes all the glory for your unfailing love and faithfulness. ²Why let the nations say, "Where is their God?" ³Our God is in the heavens, and he does as he wishes. ⁴Their idols are merely things of silver and gold, shaped by human hands. ⁵They have mouths but cannot speak, and eyes but cannot see. ⁶They have ears but cannot hear, and noses but cannot smell. ⁷They have hands but cannot feel, and feet but cannot walk, and throats but cannot make a sound. ⁸And those who make idols are just like them, as are all who trust in them.

The psalmist here lampoons those who made wood, stone, gold or silver images of their gods and then worshiped them. They would no doubt have said, as many people still do today, that they were worshipping the real god behind the image[7]. The challenge the psalmist gives is, 'Do those gods really care and show the worshippers the unfailing love and faithfulness that the Creator God demonstrated to the covenant people of Israel?' We in turn need to be careful to give God the glory for God's unfailing love and faithfulness to us.

⁹O Israel, trust the Lord! He is your helper and your shield. ¹⁰O priests, descendants of Aaron, trust the Lord! He is your helper and your shield. ¹¹All you who fear the Lord, trust the Lord! He is your helper and your shield. ¹²The Lord remembers us and will bless us.

... ¹⁴May the Lord richly bless both you and your children. ¹⁵May you be blessed by the Lord, who made heaven and earth. ... Praise the Lord!

---

[7] St. Paul in the NT went further and claimed that the only gods behind the images are demons who love to receive people's worship rather than them worshipping the Creator God.

The palmist went on to pray blessings on both Israel and all who revere the One Creator God; and to call on us all to praise the Lord God!

A poem in the theme of Psalm 115: -

O Lord God eternal,
Your justice is true:
And laced in your mercy,
Your Christ love shines through!

A prayer: Help us Lord God praise your faithfulness. Amen

PSALM 116

¹I love the LORD because he hears my voice and my prayer for mercy. ... ²Because he bends down to listen, ... ⁴I called on the name of the LORD: "Please, LORD, save me!" ⁵How kind the LORD is! How good he is! So merciful, this God of ours! ... ⁶The LORD protects those of childlike faith; I was facing death, and he saved me. ⁷Let my soul be at rest again, for the LORD has been good to me.

One of the reasons we believe is because when we have instinctively called out to the unknown for help, help has come: and so, when next we are in trouble, we have confidence to call out again to the God beyond our understanding. This embryonic faith is gradually turned into confident faith that is no longer childish, treating God as if magic, but childlike in its simplicity.

¹⁰I believed in you, so I said, "I am deeply troubled, LORD." ... ¹²What can I offer the LORD for all he has done for me? ¹³I will lift up the cup of salvation and praise the LORD's name for saving me. ¹⁴I will keep my promises to the LORD in the presence of all his people. ... ¹⁷I will offer you a sacrifice of thanksgiving and call on the name of the LORD.

Our faith is deepened by hearing the message of God transmitted through those who have trained their spiritual ears to hear God's Spirit speaking to them for the benefit of the faith community. We in turn can give testimony to the God who hears and saves us; and we must do so because it is by the witness of our mouths and lives that our faith is confirmed and established.

A poem based on Psalm 116: -

I love God because he has been my friend and helper
From early childhood he has been there,
Answering my dilemmas when I have called upon him
I praise him for his gentle loving care!

A prayer: Lord God, help me always look to you. Amen

PSALM 117

¹Praise the LORD, all you nations. Praise him, all you people of the earth. ²For his unfailing love for us is powerful; the LORD's faithfulness endures forever. Praise the LORD!

This is the shortest psalm in the Bible, but it is also one of the most universal. There is no reference to Israel – just an appeal to all humanity to praise God their creator by recognising God's powerful and faithful love and by responding to God in praise.

A poem with the theme of Psalm 117: -

Father God, Lord of All
Eternal mind of love,
Your love-mind-energy
Disperses time and space
Creating all of life,
Bringing relationship to all.
Our growing love for you
Transcends this universe!

A prayer: - Lord God may your name be found and owned in all the earth. Amen

PSALM 118

¹Give thanks to the LORD, for he is good! His faithful love endures forever. ²Let all Israel repeat: "His faithful love endures forever." ³Let Aaron's descendants, the priests, repeat: "His faithful love endures forever." ⁴Let all who fear the LORD repeat: "His faithful love endures forever." ⁵In my distress I prayed to the LORD, and the LORD answered me and set me free. ⁶The LORD is for me, so I will have no fear. What can mere people do to me? ... ⁸It is better to take refuge in the LORD than to trust in people. ¹⁰Though hostile nations surrounded ... and attacked me, I destroyed them all with the authority of the LORD. ... ¹³My enemies did their best to kill me, but the LORD rescued me. ¹⁴The LORD is my strength and my song; he has given me victory. ⋯ The strong right arm of the LORD has done glorious things! ¹⁷I will not die; instead, I will live to tell what the LORD has done.

The Psalmist was keen to get his message across. Those who have inherited a knowledge of God's promises and faithfulness must praise their God. A nation's leaders should praise the Lord God; and all who reverence God should praise God; because God answers prayer when we follow the teaching we have inherited, when a nation calls on God in their distress, and when the godly in the land pray.

King David defeated his enemies in the confidence that he fought with God's authority. We need to be careful about claiming God's authority in times of war. However, we are called to stand up with courage for righteousness and against all that demeans and oppresses other humans and creatures of this planet.

²¹I thank you for answering my prayer and giving me victory! ²²The stone that the builders rejected has now become the cornerstone. ²³This is the LORD's doing, and it is wonderful to see. ²⁴This is the day the LORD has

made. We will rejoice and be glad in it. ²⁷ The LORD is God, shining upon us. Take the sacrifice and bind it with cords on the altar. ²⁸ You are my God, and I will praise you!

The idiom used in verse 22 (see endnote) in reference to King David who at one point had been ousted from power by his rebel son, but was then restored to the throne by his faithful general. The NT points this verse out as one of the prophecies for Jesus Christ the Messiah, since the Jewish leaders had rejected him, in their jealousy condemning him to death, but God raised him up and has made him the cornerstone by which all humanity can come into the eternal relationship with God.

Verse 27 refers to the blood sacrifice that David would have offered to God in humility for his sins and in thanksgiving for his victory. Equally in thanksgiving to God, we need to accept the acceptable sacrifice of his life that Jesus offered to God not for his sins as he was sinless, but for our sins. Then we need to live in the victory that Christ has accomplished over evil in this world.

A poem based on the theme of Psalm 118: -

Father God we love you
Showing us your way
Your special presence bringing
On that first Christmas day,
Jesus Christ your present
Given for humankind
Brought in all humility
Placed for us to find
In a stable; on a cross –
Plain for all to view
Invited to encounter
To give our lives to you:
Our love to your obedience,
His heart love has won:
The light of Christ still shining

Through him your only son.
Your presence in the present
Not to walk alone
But to draw on power
Coming from above
To bless and help all others
Find your heart of love.

A prayer: - Thank you Lord God that in Christ you have overcome evil for me in this world. Help me to live in that victory. Amen

PSALM 119

A 'Joyful are those who obey God's laws and search for him with all their hearts. (Psm.119 v.2)'
There is a joy in those who live,
Seek God's way, trust him to give
All they need with thankful heart, and
With honest tongue live out their part

B 'I will delight in your decrees and not forget your words (Psm.119 v.16)'
The young in faith will need to train
Read God's law, wisdom to gain:
Find God's grace to right their flaws
And praising God walk in his laws

C 'Open my eyes to see the wonderful truths in your instructions. (Psm119 v.18)'
Awesome are your deeds Lord God
Marvellous your ways
Deep your everlasting love
And worthy of our praise!

D 'Give me understanding and I will obey your instructions; I will put them into practice with all my heart. (Psm.119 v.34)'

Open my eyes dear God to see
The hidden depths within your truth:
The wonderous things writ to inspire
To roll our sleeves, not stand aloof!

E 'LORD, give me your unfailing love, the salvation that you promised me. (Psm.119 v.41)'

God you promise salvation
To all who call upon your name
Given to all in Christ your Son
Dear Lord I ask for the same!

F 'Your promise revives me; it comforts me in all my troubles. (Psm.119 v.50)'

Thank you for your promises
I'll ponder them each day:
As they build faith in my heart,
Teach me to walk your way.

G 'O LORD, your unfailing love fills the earth; teach me your decrees. (Psm.119 v.64)'

In love and wisdom,
You have made all things
Fill my heart with love
So your wisdom grows
As I learn your ways
And so, bring you praise!

H 'I believe in your commands; now teach me good judgment and knowledge. (Psm.119 v.66)'

In all life's struggle every day
Your love Lord God is in it all.
So help me find your help each day
To live and give to you my all

Psalm 119

The Holy Psalms of David (Zabur)

J   'May all who fear you find in me a cause for joy, for I have put my hope in your word. (Psm.119 v.74)'
Everlasting joy is ours
Following his way
We're one in God's community
Welcoming each day.

K   'My eyes are straining to see your promises come true. When will you comfort me? (Psm.119 v.82)'
I cry to God his way to find.
Frustrated now I wait to see
Holding your promise God in faith
What answer Lord you give to me

L   'Your eternal word, O Lord, stands firm in heaven. (Psm.119 v.89)'
God, your eternal word stands firm
Soaring high as the mountain peaks.
With justice Lord you've made all things
Creation thus your glory speaks.

M   'How sweet your words taste to me; they are sweeter than honey. (Psm.119 v.103)'
Together with your grace of love,
I savour your words like honey:
Together with all kinds of power
Save me from the love of money.

N   'Your word is a lamp to guide my feet and a light for my path. (Psm.119 v.105)'
I am weak and fragile - spiritually poor
Turn my eyes - look forward to the path I go
Shine your light there for me - to that eternal shore
Dare I pray more Jesus, - dare I pray for more?

Psalm 119

P   LORD, sustain me as you promised, that I may live! Do not let my hope be crushed. (Psm119 v.116)
My hope is firmly fixed in God
Come whatever may:
God will be there to take me through
To his perfect day!

Q   Each of your commandments is right. That is why I hate every false way. (Psm.119 v.128)
Keep my heart from lies
My tongue from all deceit,
Your thoughts will purify
My mind to your heartbeat.

R   The teaching of your word gives light, so even the simple can understand. (Psm.119 v.130)
Your thoughts lighten up my world
So, my heart can understand
The pure heart of God within:
By God's love, my love is fanned.

S   Your promises have been thoroughly tested; that is why I love them so much. (Psm.119 v.140)
The gold standard of life
Are Your promises, dear Lord:
I love to trust in them
So, hold me by their cord.

T   I rise early, before the sun is up; I cry out for help and put my hope in your words. (Psm.119 v.147)
Early on you each day I wait
To hear your words and seek to pray,
Commit myself to live your way;
Then rise to live with joy my day!

V   L‍ORD, how great is your mercy; let me be revived by following your regulations. (Psm.119 v.156)
Revive us Lord as we seek your face
Giving our lives totally to you;
Determined now we press on to wait,
Eschewing earth's fancies while we do.

X   I rejoice in your word like one who discovers a great treasure. (Psm.119 v.162)
Holy Spirit you open up your words
To speak to me of the hidden things
God, you have placed therein to help me grow
Thank you, Lord for the pleasure that brings!

Y   Let my tongue sing about your word, for all your commands are right. (Psm.119 v.172)
Help me God, sing out your praise
With every fleeting breath your call
To come and follow the way of him
Who shone your light for one and all!

Z   'He is the Alpha and Omega (Rev.21)'
Creator God creation spoke
Giving light and life to all:
Revealed in Christ God's love redeems
To New Creation by God's Call!

A prayer: May I walk in your presence day by day. Amen

PSALM 120

The Psalms 120 to 134 inclusive, are said to be psalms for pilgrims to sing as they approached Jerusalem for the annual sacrifice.

> [1] I took my troubles to the LORD; I cried out to him, and he answered my prayer. [2] Rescue me, O LORD, from liars and from all deceitful people. [3] O deceptive tongue, what will God do to you? How will he increase your punishment? [4] You will be pierced with sharp arrows and burned with glowing coals. ... [6] I am tired of living among people who hate peace. [7] I search for peace; but when I speak of peace, they want war!

People of goodwill seek for peace. It is the proud and arrogant who love violence and war and it is the deceitful tongue that often sparks the flame of resentment that leads to self-justification of hatred and war. People of peace are people who love others, and are willingly forgive others their trespasses, while holding fast to truth and reconciliation. Religious pride is the most pernicious justifying as it does violence and discrimination against other people of different creed. God hates the lying tongue as well as the unforgiving heart. Isaiah recognised that he was a sinner whose heart and lips were unclean and, in a vision, he saw God's angel touch his lips and cleanse his heart with a burning coal from God's throne (Isa.Ch.6 v.6&7). The Psalmist speaks in verse 4 of those unlike Isaiah who don't repent of their deceitful hearts and lips – it is the same fire of God, the metaphorical 'burning coals,' that purifies the repentant and consumes the unrepentant in judgement.

A Poem from Psalm 120: -
O purify my lips that I may speak your praise
Cleanse my heart of self-pride and arrogance:
Lord God, I trust your grace to save me from deceit
And to cloth me in your truth and fragrance!

A prayer: Help me worship You Lord God in truth. Amen

PSALM 121

A song for pilgrims ascending to Jerusalem.

¹ **I look up to the mountains— does my help come from there?** ² **My help comes from the LORD, who made heaven and earth!** ...

The Psalmist asks the rhetorical question, 'Does my help come from the hills?' To which he knew the answer was, 'No!' This was because tribes in the ancient Middle East did not settle in the valleys as they might do in peaceful areas of the world, but on hilltops which could be more easily defended from enemies; and so, the surrounding hills were as likely to house your enemies as your friends. Rather the Psalmist looked to the Lord God in faith for his help.

⁴ **Indeed, he who watches over Israel never slumbers or sleeps.** ⁵ **The LORD himself watches over you! The LORD stands beside you as your protective shade.** ⁶ **The sun will not harm you by day, nor the moon at night.** ⁷ **The LORD keeps you from all harm and watches over your life.** ⁸ **The LORD keeps watch over you as you come and go, both now and forever.**

Just as the shade of a rock outcrop can protect you from the heat of the midday sun, and a secure home will protect you from wild animals that prowl around in the moonlight looking for a kill, so the Psalmist likens the protection afforded to those who trust in the Lord God from those who would harm them openly in the world and those who would harm them when they are vulnerable and least aware.

A poem based on Psalm 121: -

The Lord is my defence by day
And my security by night.
Because I place my trust in God.
I will not fear those who attack
Openly or behind my back

Prayer: I will not fear with you dear Lord beside me! Amen.

PSALM 122

¹I was glad when they said to me, "Let us go to the house of the LORD." ²And now here we are, standing inside your gates, O Jerusalem. ... ⁴All the tribes of Israel—the LORD's people— make their pilgrimage here. They come to give thanks to the name of the LORD ...

This is reminiscent of the city of God in the Book of Revelation: *'¹Then I saw a new heaven and a new earth, for the old heaven and the old earth had disappeared. ...²And I saw the holy city, the new Jerusalem, coming down from God out of heaven like a bride beautifully dressed for her husband ... ²²I saw no temple in the city, for the Lord God Almighty and the Lamb are its temple. ²³ And the city has no need of sun or moon, for the glory of God illuminates the city, and the Lamb is its light. ²⁴ The nations will walk in its light, and the kings of the world will enter the city in all their glory ²⁵ Its gates will never be closed at the end of day because there is no night there. ²⁶ And all the nations will bring their glory and honour into the city. ²⁷ Nothing evil will be allowed to enter, nor anyone who practices shameful idolatry and dishonesty—but only those whose names are written in the Lamb's Book of Life. (Rev.21 v.1,2 & 22-27).'*

⁶Pray for peace in Jerusalem. May all who love this city prosper. ⁷O Jerusalem, may there be peace within your walls and prosperity in your palaces. ⁸For the sake of my family and friends, I will say, "May you have peace." ⁹For the sake of the house of the LORD our God, I will seek what is best for you, O Jerusalem.

The NT confirms the wisdom of these verses when we are told **to** *'pray for all those in authority so that we may lead a quiet and peaceable life in all godliness – for this is good and acceptable in the sight of God ...' (1 Tim.2 v.2&3).*

The psalmist understood that the worship of God is tied to the peace of the community and the stability of its leadership.

A poem: -

Dear God, we pray for all those in authority
That we may live peaceful lives and pursue
Righteous ways in all humility, worshipping you,
To whom alone all praise from us is due!

A prayer: I love you Lord; you alone are my strength and shield! Amen

PSALM 123

¹ I lift my eyes to you, O God, enthroned in heaven. ² We keep looking to the LORD our God for his mercy, just as servants keep their eyes on their master, as a slave girl watches her mistress for the slightest signal. ³ Have mercy on us, LORD, have mercy, for we have had our fill of contempt. ⁴ We have had more than our fill of the scoffing of the proud and the contempt of the arrogant.

Jesus taught his disciples that we should not expect any better treatment from those who know not of God's love in Christ our Lord, than that which he suffered at the hands of his persecutors.

A poem: -

Have mercy Lord, it's beyond a joke
Their persecution is unrelenting
Yet our witness is ever to you
We will love despite their constant taunting

A prayer: The Lord God shares all my pain. Amen

`PSALM 124

[1] Let all Israel repeat: [2] What if the LORD had not been on our side when people attacked us? [3] They would have swallowed us alive in their burning anger. ...[5] Yes, the raging waters of their fury would have overwhelmed our very lives. [6] Praise the LORD, who did not let their teeth tear us apart! [7] We escaped like a bird from a hunter's trap. The trap is broken, and we are free! [8] Our help is from the LORD, who made heaven and earth.

This is another pilgrim song that comments on religious persecution and gives testimony to God's faithfulness to those who suffer for their faith. Yes, there is today much burning hatred from zealots blazed against those who demonstrate a peace that emanates from God presence, beyond the experience of these zealots.

A Poem from Psalm 124: -

O Source of the peace and love that flows to those
Who rest themselves in You,
Dear God in Christ who meekly showed the way
Help us in him be true!

A prayer: I commit my soul to God in Christ. Amen

PSALM 125

[1] Those who trust in the LORD are as secure as Mount Zion; they will not be defeated but will endure forever. [2] Just as the mountains surround Jerusalem, so the LORD surrounds his people, both now and forever. [3] The wicked will not rule the land of the godly, for then the godly might be tempted to do wrong.

⁴O LORD, do good to those who are good, whose hearts are in tune with you. ⁵But banish those who turn to crooked ways, O LORD. Take them away with those who do evil! May Israel have peace!

Sadly, even ancient Israel spent more years under the rule of ungodly and wicked kings than under the rule of those who revered and loved the Lord their God. The world is little different today. Even the more apparently theocratic nations are often heavily corrupt and persecute their minorities and those of other religions, or turn a blind eye to discrimination against the defenceless. However, as the Psalmist says of those who firmly commit themselves to the revealed God of love, truth, mercy and justice, 'they will be secure in who they are (v.1)' even if they have to suffer the consequences of ungodly authorities. And they will stand firm in the strength God gives them.

A Poem from Psalm 125: -
O God of the defenceless
Give them justice and your strength.
Give them hope, faith, love, and cause
Their persecutors to relent.

A prayer: Lord help me stand against injustice and support the poor.

PSALM 126

¹When the LORD brought back his exiles to Jerusalem, it was like a dream! ²We were filled with laughter, and we sang for joy. And the other nations said, "What amazing things the LORD has done for them."

This psalm was written after the people of Israel were allowed to return to Jerusalem from exile in Babylon (after the Babylonians were defeated by the Persian king Artaxerxes). They saw this return from exile as a testimony to God's faithfulness to them.

³Yes, the LORD has done amazing things for us! What joy! ⁴Restore our fortunes, LORD, as streams renew the desert. ⁵Those who plant in tears will harvest with shouts of joy. ⁶They weep as they go to plant their seed, but they sing as they return with the harvest.

Recalling the miracle of national restoration would have encouraged the returnees in the work of ploughing fallow land, sowing crops and re-building homesteads that had been abandoned. The hope of a new and better future gave impetus to the hard work involved. It is labelled as a song of ascents for pilgrims to sing as they climbed up to Jerusalem. It reminds us that whatever is worth doing, is worth doing well. And if we want to offer our toil or goods to God in thanksgiving, then it should not cost us nothing - we need to have put our own effort and love into it. This is reminiscent of the Hebrew festival of Shelters (Jewish Sukkot) when the ex-slaves reflected on the temporality of life and rejoiced after bringing in the late harvest. It was a time of joy and celebration and reminds us that God rejoices over all those who have turned from their own self-centred ways and instead embraced a life of loving God and all others.

A poem from Psalm 126: -

Praise the Lord the day will come
When all are gathered in harvest song
Freed from slavery to sin
Who for others toiled and lived
Ruled by God's love and now redeemed
Forever with all God's kin.

A Prayer: Dear Lord God help me believe and give to you my love that you may use me in your kingdom. Amen

PSALM 127

This is another pilgrims' song, but is one with a teaching message rather than a worship song. The first verse reminds us that all our work should be an outworking of God's work in and through us rather than us striving in our own strength (as the previous psalm indicates). This doesn't mean that we don't have to put our best effort into it – we must, but also asking God for strength while we do it.

> ¹**Unless the LORD builds a house, the work of the builders is wasted. Unless the LORD protects a city, guarding it with sentries will do no good. ²It is useless for you to work so hard from early morning until late at night, anxiously working for food to eat; for God gives rest to his loved ones.**

Verse 2 is a reminder for us not to be over-anxious. Our work should be offered to God and not motivated for our own glory, remembering that God has also ordained us to both work and rest – so we must enjoy our rest-times.

> ³**Children are a gift from the LORD; they are a reward from him. ⁴Children born to a young man are like arrows in a warrior's hands. ⁵How joyful is the man whose quiver is full of them! He will not be put to shame when he confronts his accusers at the city gates.**

The psalm ends on an encouraging message for parents to enjoy their children and not to put off having them while you are still in your vital years.

A poem from Psalm 127: -

> *Eternal God so guide my daily round*
> *That I may trust your grace to live each day*
> *And in your peace direct my thought and hand,*
> *So, I rejoice content in rest to lay!*

A prayer: I thank you God for family, may your peace dwell there. Amen

PSALM 128

¹How joyful are those who fear the Lord – all who follow his ways! ²You will enjoy the fruit of your labour. How joyful and prosperous you will be! ³Your wife will be like a fruitful grapevine, flourishing within your home. Your children will be like vigorous young olive trees as they sit around your table. ⁴That is the Lord's blessing for those who fear him. ⁵May the Lord continually bless you from Zion ... ⁶May you live to enjoy your grandchildren. May Israel have peace!

This song of ascent for pilgrims spells out the blessing for those 'who follow God's ways (v.1),' i.e., those who love and reverence God. But it must be noted well that these promises (blessings for family life, work and security) are all relative. Jesus also reminded us that those who love God will have blessings but not without the persecutions and rejection from the world that doesn't know or love God. Nor should we think that the blessings we have are the guaranteed result of our righteousness. God can give and God can take away – as St. Paul exclaimed, he had learnt to be content (and even rejoice) in both plenty and in want! The psalm ends with prayers (v.5, 6) inclusive of a prayer for the peace of the land where the pilgrims lived. We should always pray the same for the lands where we live. We can never take peace for granted.

Those who truly love God will follow his commandments and will show love to other people (even their enemies) with the same generosity they show themselves. Such love flows only from a deep appreciation of God's love for us. As the NT declares, **'God shows his love for us in that, while we were still sinners, Christ died for us (Rom.5 v.8).'**

A poem on the theme of Psalm 128: -

Give God your thoughts, your hurts, your pain;
Trust him to heal your wounds
Ask God to gently lead your way
Help you to find the runes
That open up your door to life
To live in peace each day.
Since God has come in Jesus Christ
God will show you his way!
Then, peace of mind and heart and tongue
Will fill your life anew;
Purpose, love, hope, and self-respect
And joy break out in you! MJK

A prayer: - Dear Lord God, I respect your love, help me joyful be. Amen

PSALM 129

¹Let all Israel repeat this: '²From my earliest youth my enemies have persecuted me, but they have never defeated me.' ³My back is covered with cuts, as if a farmer had ploughed long furrows. ⁴But the Lord is good; he has cut me free from the ropes of the ungodly. ⁵May all who hate Jerusalem be turned back in shameful defeat. ...

Although those who worship the Creator God in Christ Jesus will from time to time suffer persecutions, they can expect the Lord God not to allow them to be overwhelmed by their oppressors. This psalm speaks into the historical experience of the Jewish nation from Abraham to the Messiah Jesus and it is also prophetic of the life of Jesus himself who 'gave his back to the lashings of the Roman scourge and crucifixion, but was not defeated since God then raised him from the dead!

We too can trust God to enable us never to be defeated even though we *'pass through the shadow of the valley of death (Psalm 23 v.4).'*

A poem from Psalm 129: -

Lord God, they persecuted you in Christ.
Jesus showed the way to love all others,
Yet, not fight back: take our wounds to you in prayer,
To love others as mothers, sisters, brothers

A prayer: Lord God, may the Spirit of Christ help me pray for those who may persecute me. Amen

PSALM 130

This song of a pilgrim ascending to Jerusalem starts as a prayer for deliverance from despair (v.1 & 2), and then makes some very profound statements about God.

'**³Lord if you had kept a record of our sins, who, O Lord, could ever survive? ⁴But you offer forgiveness, that we might learn to fear you.**'

The Hebrew word translated as 'fear' in verse 4, means 'loving reverence' i.e., God's offer of merciful forgiveness (v.4) aims to bring us to a relationship of loving reverence for God, or in New Testament terms 'to bring us into a healthy personal relationship with our Saviour God'. The pilgrim recognises that we have no righteousness of our own to approach the all-holy creator God, but that God reaches out to us offering us completely unmerited forgiveness simply so that we might learn to love and respect God. This is a message of hope and of God's grace – the hope we need that lifts us from despair.

Have you realised with the Psalmist that nothing you can do will ever earn you an audience with God; and that you need to accept his overflowing mercy that offers forgiveness?

> '⁵I am counting on the Lord; yes, I am counting on him. I have put my hope in his word.'

This heart revealing prayer shows that this pilgrim clings only to God's promises. He is not counting on his own efforts to somehow please God. Instead, he is counting on God's promises.

Jesus told a story of two men who went to the temple to pray. One a self-righteous religious leader, the other a despised tax collector. The religious man thanked God he was not like the despised tax collector and recounted all his good works to God. The tax collector in despair however, cried out for God to be merciful to him a sinner. Jesus then challenged his audience as to which man left the temple knowing God's peace and forgiveness. And Jesus answered his own question stating it was the tax collector who left the temple justified in God's sight!

Do you know and trust in God's promises given especially to us in the New Testament?

> '⁷O Israel, hope in the Lord; for with the Lord there is unfailing love... ⁸He himself will redeem Israel from every kind of sin

This psalm was penned by a Jewish pilgrim who ends by calling on his nation to hope in God's redeeming grace, i.e., God's will and power to change the hearts and lives of all who want to turn from their sinfulness and live lives that please God. And this plea is applicable to people of all nations and creeds.

A poem from Psalm 130: -

> *Lord God on my righteousness I can't rely*
> *But only on your sovereign grace.*
> *For mercy based on Christ's righteousness alone,*
> *I seek the love to see your face.*

A prayer: Lord God, you have shown me that Jesus is the way, the truth and the life of your grace. Amen

PSALM 131

'¹Lord, my heart is not proud; my eyes are not haughty. I don't concern myself with matters too great or too awesome for me to grasp. ²Instead, I have calmed and quieted myself, like a weaned child who no longer cries for its mother's milk. Yes, like a weaned child is my soul within me. ³O Israel, put your hope in the Lord— now and always.'

This psalm has echoes of Psalm 46, where in verse ten, the Psalmist calls us to *'Be still and know that the Lord is God.'* This is a good attitude (combined with a thankful heart) in which to approach God in prayer.

A poem from Psalm 131: -

Lord God I now wait for you
In the quietness of my soul:
Speak patiently to my being
So, your peace will make me whole.

A prayer: Merciful and forgiving Father God, teach me quietness in my heart.

PSALM 132

A song for pilgrims ascending to the temple in Jerusalem.

¹Lord remember David and all that he suffered. ²He made a solemn promise to the Lord. He vowed to the Mighty One of Israel, ... ⁴"I will not let myself rest ... ⁵until I find a place to build a house for the Lord, a sanctuary for the Mighty One of Israel." ...

⁶We heard that the Ark was in Ephrathah; then we found it in the distant countryside of Jaar. ⁷Let us go to the sanctuary of the Lord; let us worship at the footstool of his throne. ⁸Arise, O Lord, and enter your resting place, along with the ark, the symbol of your power

The Holy Psalms of David (Zabur)

The psalm reflects on how the Jerusalem temple became the focus of worship for Jewish pilgrims. It starts with king David vowing to build God a place of worship where the ark of the covenant between the Jewish nation and Jehovah God could be kept. The ark of the 'covenant' was a sacred box containing the ten commandments given to Moses and carried the 'Mercy seat' as its lid. The High Priest would enter the inner sanctuary once a year to make atonement for the sins of the people and would sprinkle the blood of the atonement sacrifice on the Mercy seat to seal God's forgiveness of his people.

God's covenant was conditional on the Israelites (led by their king) faithfully obeying Jehovah; and the ark was the symbol of God's presence with his people. Hence this psalm in verse 6, speaks of the time when the ark which had been lost in battle to the Philistines, found its way back to Israel and was then brought back to Jerusalem by King David. David had then planned to build a temple to house the ark so God's presence could rest in Jerusalem. However, the temple was not built until after his death by his son King Solomon.

The psalm continues with poetic imagery linking the footsteps of the pilgrims with the time when the ark was brought to Jerusalem and finally put into the temple. It is as if the pilgrims are bringing God's presence with them as they come to worship at the temple. Although they believed they would experience God's presence when they arrived at the temple to worship, by recalling the arc's journey alongside their own journey, they were inspiring hope in their hearts that they would meet with God when they got there.

In our own era, we too need to find times and places to come away from the world and seek God's presence to renew our lives. To do this we need to take time to find inspiration and solitude with God whatever our circumstance, and a place where we can personally meet with the living God who forgives sins and calls us to live godly lives.

Psalm 132

[9]**May your priests be clothed in godliness; may your loyal servants sing for joy. **[10]**For the sake of your servant David, do not reject the king you have anointed.**

The psalm moves on to some important prayers for their nation. First is a prayer for the godliness of those appointed to represent God at the temple. This is essential for the glory of God needs to be reflected in his servants especially God's priests as a witness to the Lord's character. Then there is a twofold prayer for the people represented by those making the pilgrimage followed by a prayer for the nation's ruler (v.10). God's protection of the ruler is based on God's covenant promise to the nation. If the king is faithful to God's covenant terms, the covenant promises God's protection to the nation (v.11 to 14). The pilgrims are loyal servants coming to worship and singing songs of joy. And their prayer is that they will remain loyal to God and that their songs will be meaningful and joyous because God has clothed them with salvation (represented by the peace of Jerusalem).

A poem based on Psalm 132: -

Come with us Divine Lord
Meet with us on the way.
We set aside our times
To worship and to pray:
Keep our priests and rulers
In righteous ways this day.

A prayer: Do not forsake our nations Lord we pray. Amen

PSALM 133

Said to be a Psalm of David and used for pilgrimage

[1] **How wonderful and pleasant it is when brothers live together in harmony!** [2] **For harmony is as precious as the anointing oil that was poured over Aaron's head, that ran down his beard and onto the border of his robe.** [3] **Harmony is as refreshing as the dew from Mount Hermon that falls on the mountains of Zion. And there the LORD has pronounced his blessing, even life everlasting.**

Harmony and unity are the promise and work of God's Spirit in his people, who as the New Testament (Ingil) states should at all times 'make every effort to live at peace with everyone (Rom.12 v.18 & Heb.12 v.14).' Clearly it is the will of God that believers should work to be in harmony with each other and to live at peace with all their neighbours. In a sinful world where people fail to draw on the help of God's Spirit, harmony is not always achievable, in which case the believer must agree to disagree graciously, but without becoming judgemental, resentful or bitter.

As the Psalmist declares (v.3) where humanity works to live together in peace, God blesses those communities.

A poem based on Psalm 133: -

Holy Spirit of God
Give us generous hearts
To live through all our days
With both friend and foe
In peace the best we can,
Reflecting your true ways!

A prayer: Lord God help me as far as I can, to live at peace with everyone. Amen

PSALM 134

¹ Oh, praise the LORD, all you servants of the LORD, you who serve at night in the house of the LORD. ² Lift your hands toward the sanctuary, and praise the LORD. ³ May the LORD, who made heaven and earth, bless you from Jerusalem.

This is the last of the fifteen Songs of Ascents; it is thought to be one the pilgrims sang as they left Jerusalem to go home and verse three sends them on their way with God's blessing. The psalm starts with the pilgrims calling on the permanent temple servants and priests to be always wholeheartedly and earnestly praising God in all their duties through both the day and the night.

The New Testament (Ingil) speaks of all who have received God's redemption (the forgiveness of sins and indwelling of God's Spirit) as being 'royal priests' in God's sight (1 Pet.2 v.9): consequently, this psalm of David applied to today's pilgrims calls on all the 'redeemed' to be actively and always giving honour and praise to God their Saviour throughout their lives!

A poem of blessing reflecting Psalm 134: -

Let the redeemed of the Lord
Speak out God's praise
Earnestly, joyously
All of their days!

A prayer: Thank you Divine Lord God for your saving grace. Amen

PSALM 135

¹Praise the LORD! Praise the name of the LORD! Praise him, you who serve the LORD, ²you who serve in the house of the LORD ...³Praise the LORD, for the LORD is good; celebrate his lovely name with music. ⁴For the LORD has chosen Jacob for himself, Israel for his own special treasure.

Despite his limited understanding of the Lord God of all creation, the Psalmist here is filled with praise and calls us to celebrate the lovely name of God with music; a tradition practiced by Jews and Christians especially! His view of the Jews as God's own special treasure needs to be seen in context. Even in the Jewish Scriptures, God promised Abraham that through one of his Jewish decedents all the nations of the world would be blessed. And the Scripture declares that this promise is fulfilled in and through Jesus Christ.

⁵I know the greatness of the LORD—that our Lord is greater than any other god. ... ⁹He performed miraculous signs and wonders in Egypt against Pharaoh and all his people. ...¹⁵The idols of the nations are merely things of silver and gold, shaped by human hands. ¹⁶They have mouths but cannot speak, and eyes but cannot see ... ¹⁸And those who make idols are just like them, as are all who trust in them. ¹⁹O Israel, praise the LORD! ... All you who fear the LORD, praise the LORD!

The Psalmist lived in an era when other nations worshipped gods personified in idols of stone and wood. These gods were believed to have various powers (some more universal than others) that demanded acts of worship and sacrifice, but none of them matched the revealed character of the Lord of creation that Israel knew.

The character of Creator God as love, justice and mercy is fully revealed in the person of Jesus Christ. Some religions other than Christianity and Judaism also speak of the God of Creation as the God of justice and mercy, but they don't necessarily know of the One and Only intimate Creator and Sustaining God as the one who **_loves_** each and every created being and invites each of us to draw on his Spirit to enable us to live in God's character.

A Christian hymn reflecting the love of Almighty God: -
> *O Lord God eternal*
> *Your justice is true*
> *And laced in your mercy*
> *Your Christ love shines through*

A prayer: Lord God, I love you because You first loved me!

PSALM 136

[1] Give thanks to the LORD, for he is good! ... [4] Give thanks to him who alone does mighty miracles. *His faithful love endures forever.*
[5] Give thanks to him who made the heavens so skilfully... [11] He brought Israel out of Egypt. *His faithful love endures forever.*
[16] Give thanks to him who led his people through the wilderness ... [23] He remembered us in our weakness. *His faithful love endures forever. ...*
[25] He gives food to every living thing ... [26] Give thanks to the God of heaven. *His faithful love endures forever.*

A hymn reflecting praise to God for his love and faithfulness:
> *O Creator God, we are your people*
> *You love us with an everlasting love!*
> *You call us to your eternal kingdom:*
> *And make us your people of praise!*

A prayer: Dear Lord and Father of humankind, teach us what your love means for us. Amen

PSALM 137

¹ Beside the rivers of Babylon, we sat and wept as we thought of Jerusalem. ² We put away our harps, hanging them on the branches of poplar trees. ³ For our captors demanded a song from us. Our tormentors insisted on a joyful hymn ... ⁴ But how can we sing the songs of the LORD while in a pagan land?

The Psalmist asks an emotional question in verses 3 & 4 about how the exiles could sing God's praises in a foreign land. But he then addresses his own question in verses 5 & 6. Whatever our feelings we must still focus on singing God's praises even in a foreign land because it keeps us drawing down on strength we need from God's Spirit!

⁵ If I forget you, O Jerusalem, let my right hand forget how to play the harp. ⁶ May my tongue stick to the roof of my mouth if I fail to remember you, if I don't make Jerusalem my greatest joy.

Sadly, the Psalmist then gives vent to his emotions about the revenge he would like to see poured out on their Babylonian captors.

⁷ O LORD, remember ... the day the armies of Babylon captured Jerusalem. "Destroy it!" they yelled ... ⁸ O Babylon, you will be destroyed. Happy is the one who pays you back for what you have done to us...

This sentiment might be understandable, but it is not in line with the Spirit of God expressed through Jesus Christ who in God's love forgave those enemies who nailed him to a cruel Roman cross. We need to find God's grace to love our enemies.

A poem based on Psalm 137: -
May we acknowledge our feelings Lord
But not give them the air for violence:
Whatever they say, may we hear your Word
And construct our actions with innocence!

A prayer: Lord help us show love to our enemies. Amen

PSALM 138

Attributed to King David, this psalm speaks of his bold witness to the One God Jehovah made before the surrounding nations, their kings and their gods. It speaks of his confidence that God will use his witness to enlighten the pagan kings around him.

¹I give you thanks, O LORD, with all my heart; I will sing your praises before the gods. ²I bow before your holy Temple as I worship. I praise your name for your unfailing love and faithfulness; for your promises are backed by all the honour of your name. ³As soon as I pray, you answer me; you encourage me by giving me strength. ⁴Every king in all the earth will thank you, LORD, for all of them will hear your words. ⁵Yes, they will sing about the LORD's ways, for the glory of the LORD is very great. ⁶Though the LORD is great, he cares for the humble, but he keeps his distance from the proud.

David was aware of his own relative humility before God who had saved him in the midst of many troubles both before and after becoming king of Israel. This didn't mean he was perfect as his sin relating to Bathsheba illustrated. But his imperfections didn't prevent him from declaring the praises of God, nor should our imperfections discourage us from doing the same!

⁷Though I am surrounded by troubles, you will protect me from the anger of my enemies. You reach out your hand, and the power of your right hand saves me. ⁸The LORD will work out his plans for my life— for your faithful love, O LORD, endures forever. Don't abandon me, for you made me.

In verse 3, David only stated that as soon as he prayed God started to strengthen him. He was not saying that God answered all his prayers or that God did so immediately, as many other psalms of David's demonstrate.

A poem based on Psalm 138: -
Lord God you are worthy of my praise
Though I'm not worthy so to give;
Yet you have mercy on my plight
And cause your grace in me to live.

A prayer: God, have your way in me, I pray

PSALM 139

[1] O Lord, you have examined my heart and know everything about me. ... [3] You see me when I travel and when I rest at home. You know everything I do. [4] You know what I am going to say even before I say it, Lord. ... [5] You place your hand of blessing on my head. [6] Such knowledge is too wonderful for me, too great for me to understand! [7] I can never escape from your Spirit ... [8] If I go up to heaven, you are there; if I go down to the grave, you are there. [9] If I ride the wings of the morning, if I dwell by the farthest oceans, [10] even there your hand will guide me, and your strength will support me.

God presently supports the very 'web and woof' of all creation, desiring for every creature to reach its full potential, for every human to transcend their rightful business with God-inspired love and sacrifice. God gives us freedom and God also sees the good and the evil that we can unleash. God suffers with those we harm, but God rejoices when we choose to follow His Spirit in sacrificial love. Since God knows all our conversation (v.3 & 4), we should be quick to listen and slow to speak!

The Psalmist declared how close God is to everyone one of us (v.7-10) and to all of nature. Whether or not we realise it and in ways beyond our comprehension, God is closer than our breath and God's Spirit encourages us towards our full potential. He is not implying that this potential (whether our own or that of nature) will be reached unaided– there is always ambiguity in creation – but he is saying that God is always there to help us respond in a God-aided manner if we so choose.

> [13]You made all the delicate, inner parts of my body and knit me together in my mother's womb. [14]Thank you for making me so wonderfully complex! ... [15]You watched me as I was being formed in utter seclusion ... [16]You saw me before I was born. Every day of my life was recorded in your book. [17]How precious are your thoughts about me, O God.

The Psalmist wondered with thankfulness at the marvels of the human body and of God's motherly love for his own creation. He postulated that God sees our whole life; the end from the beginning without interfering with our free will. Since God knows and loves us intimately with all our personality traits and our imperfections, we should surely trust him in all circumstances?!

David then went on to reflect on God's omniscience (v.16). We are not robots; we are free to make our own way in life, but God sees the choices we will make and remains willing to guide us if we call on him, but God respects our free choices. However, God's Spirit is always there for us to call on day by day (v.7 & 8).

> [19]O God, if only you would destroy the wicked! Get out of my life, you murderers! ... [21]O Lord, shouldn't I hate those who hate you? ... [23]Search me, O God, and know my heart; test me and know my anxious thoughts. [24]Point out anything in me that offends you, and lead me along the path of everlasting life.

The Psalmist then asked a pertinent question (v.21). Should he not hate those who hate God and what God stands for? It seems he had doubts about this and then exposed these doubts further by asking God to examine his own motives. He was conscious that he wasn't perfect either.

Jesus Christ who was the only perfect human (according to both the Holy Bible and Qur'an) stated that we should all love our enemies (not hate them) since God also desires that they should come to repentance.

Poem from Psalm 139: -
Love Divine closer than my breath
You know all that there is to know.
You know my DNA, my thoughts,
The character my deeds will sow:
And by your grace what I can be,
And the way that I will choose to go.

Prayer: O Lord, help me share your passion that even my enemies should turn to you and come to share in your eternal love. Amen

PSALM 140

The psalmist here was wrestling with the problem of evil[8].

1 O LORD, rescue me from evil people. Protect me from those who are violent, 2 those who plot evil in their hearts and stir up trouble all day long. ... 4 O LORD, keep me out of the hands of the wicked. ... 5 The proud have set a trap to catch me; they have stretched out a net; they have placed traps all along the way. 6 I said to the LORD, "You are my God!" Listen, O LORD, to my cries for mercy! ... 8 LORD, do not let evil people have their way. Do not let their evil schemes succeed, or they will become proud. 9 Let my enemies be destroyed by the very evil they have planned for me. ... 11 Don't let liars prosper here in our land. Cause great disasters to fall on the violent.

---

[8] See End Note on Psalm 140 for further discussion on the problem of evil

¹² But I know the L**ORD**** will help those they persecute; he will give justice to the poor. ¹³ Surely righteous people are praising your name; the godly will live in your presence.**

How would you define evil? Undoubtedly it is manifest in and through the human heart where its strongest protagonists are pride and deceit. It is those who are proud-hearted (v.5) who often want to gain power over others, or to set themselves up to receive the admiration of others. And it is these same people who create lies (v.11) to achieve their goals, and, where they can get away with it, use violence (v.1) as well. The same people are inclined to peddle conspiracy theories and fake news to water-down or conceal the truth and they lay traps to bring down the righteous (v.2,5).

How are those who despite their own failings are nevertheless committed to openness, serving others and to the welfare of all people, to defend themselves against such evil? The psalmist here gives us some clues: viz., Prayer and God-dependency (v.1, 4, 6-8); leaving all vengeance in God's hands (v.9, 12); and seeking to live in God (v.13). In the New Testament, Paul adds a further means to stand up to and overcome evil that wasn't available to King David, that of the Gospel of Jesus (2 Cor.10 v.3-5). The spiritual weapons Paul speaks of are those words from God that by prayer penetrate to the heart and truth of issues and expose the false paradigms that people cling to in order to justify their way of life.

Poem based on Psalm 140: -

Lord help me overcome evil with good
As I look to you to defend my cause.
Keep me from resentful unworthy thoughts;
Save me from the oppressor's schemes and jaws!

Prayer: *Lord God I would put on the armour of Christ who prayed for the welfare of his enemies. Amen*

PSALM 141

¹O Lord, I am calling to you. ... ³Take control of what I say, O LORD, and guard my lips. ⁴Don't let me drift toward evil or take part in acts of wickedness. Don't let me share in the delicacies of those who do wrong. ⁵Let the godly strike me! It will be a kindness! If they correct me, it is soothing medicine. Don't let me refuse it.

David was at times aware of the temptations: to be careless in what we say (v3); to drift into ungodly ways and enjoy the fruits of wickedness (v.4). And he was aware that the godly must be open to and welcome the challenge of correction (v.5). David notably repented as soon as the prophet Nathan exposed his sin over Bathsheba and her husband. How willing are we to respond to the rebuke of another as iron sharpens iron? Jesus taught we must first remove the plank from our own eye before we attempt to correct another, however, this should not stop the godly in humility challenging a brother or sister who has fallen below their vows before God and others.

... But I pray constantly against the wicked and their deeds. ⁶When their leaders are thrown down from a cliff, the wicked will listen to my words and find them true. ... ⁹Keep me from the traps they have set for me, from the snares of those who do wrong. ¹⁰Let the wicked fall into their own nets, but let me escape.

David concluded the psalm by ruefully commenting that in his experience it takes the fall of the leaders they trust in before the ungodly begin to listen to the correction of the godly. He then prayed for God to protect him from the wicked.

Poem based on Psalm 141: -
Lord help me take care how I speak,
Accept rebuke and listen well.
Keep me from all ungodly ways,
And help my life proclaim your praise!
Prayer: Lord keep me from the snare of my enemies. Amen

PSALM 142

¹ I cry out to the LORD; I plead for the LORD's mercy. ² I pour out my complaints before him and tell him all my troubles. ³ When I am overwhelmed, you alone know the way I should turn. Wherever I go, my enemies have set traps for me. ⁴ I look for someone to come and help me, but no one gives me a passing thought! No one will help me; no one cares a bit what happens to me. ⁵ Then I pray to you, O LORD. I say, "You are my place of refuge. You are all I really want in life. ⁶ Hear my cry, for I am very low. Rescue me from my persecutors, for they are too strong for me. ⁷ Bring me out of prison so I can thank you. The godly will crowd around me, for you are good to me."

This psalm is believed to be a prayer David composed about his time of escaping from King Saul and his forces when he was forced to hide in a deep cave. The psalmist certainly sounds very despondent reflecting the feelings we often may feel when things seem set against us and nothing is going the way we think it should. But he did the right thing in that he turned his situation over to God in whom he trusted, and God who in time did deliver him for all his woes.

This also reminds us that even when God doesn't answer our prayers in the way and at the time we expect, we must nevertheless hold on to our faith in God's love and good purposes for us.

Poem based on Psalm 142: -

Lord help me turn to you in prayer
And cast my burdens on to you
Since you are gracious and will hear
And help me to find your way through.

Prayer: God I trust you, help me wait for you. Amen

PSALM 143

¹ Hear my prayer, O LORD; listen to my plea! Answer me because you are faithful and righteous. ² Don't put your servant on trial, for no one is innocent before you. ³ My enemy has chased me. He has knocked me to the ground and forces me to live in darkness like those in the grave. ⁴ I am losing all hope; I am paralyzed with fear. ⁵ I remember the days of old. I ponder all your great works and think about what you have done. ⁶ I lift my hands to you in prayer. I thirst for you as parched land thirsts for rain.

⁷ Come quickly, LORD, and answer me, for my depression deepens. Don't turn away from me, or I will die. ⁸ Let me hear of your unfailing love each morning, for I am trusting you. Show me where to walk, for I give myself to you. ⁹ Rescue me from my enemies, LORD; I run to you to hide me. ¹⁰ Teach me to do your will, for you are my God. May your gracious Spirit lead me forward on a firm footing. ¹¹ For the glory of your name, O LORD, preserve my life. Because of your faithfulness, bring me out of this distress. ¹² In your unfailing love, silence all my enemies and destroy all my foes, for I am your servant.

This is another psalm of David (similar in vein to Psalms 42 & 142), where David recognised and admitted his low mood of hopelessness (4) and depression (7).

And David took several good positive steps in this and other psalms to put himself on track to winning back control of his faith and overcoming his depression.

1. He recognised his low emotional/ mental/ spiritual condition and lifted his situation up to God in prayer (143 v.6).
2. He recognised that fear (probably of his enemy King Saul at this venture) was paralysing him from action including making wise decisions (143 v.4).
3. He addressed his fear by remembering previous times when he had experienced God's presence and enabling (v.5). and had known God's love (143 v.8).
4. He surrendered his will to God and waited for God to direct his actions (142 v.5; 143 v.8).
5. He spoke to himself about God's promises (42 v.8).
6. He sang out God's praises (42 v.11).

We would do well to follow David's example when faced with sapping opposition, danger and/ or depression. God often takes his servants through testing times to prepare them for greater opportunity in service (e.g., in the lives of Moses, Job, David, et al). In dong so their faith is strengthened for greater service!

Poem based on Psalm 143: -

In danger and uncertainty,
  teach me God to turn to you;
Admit my fear, lay down my way,
  give you Lord my life anew.
Help me to think of all your deeds,
  remember those better days;
And wait on you to lead my way,
  and then give you all the praise!

Prayer: Holy Spirit help me be still and know that God is Lord.

Psalm 144

PSALM 144

In this acrostic psalm, David gives credit to God for his skill in battle and helping him expand the kingdom of Israel.

¹ Praise the LORD, who is my rock. He trains my hands for war and gives my fingers skill for battle. ² He is my loving ally and my fortress, my tower of safety, my rescuer. He is my shield, and I take refuge in him. He makes the nations submit to me.

³ O LORD, what are human beings that you should notice them, mere mortals that you should think about them? ⁴ For they are like a breath of air; their days are like a passing shadow. ⁵ Open the heavens, LORD, and come down. Touch the mountains so they billow smoke. ⁶ Hurl your lightning bolts and scatter your enemies! ...

⁹ I will sing a new song to you, O God! I will sing your praises with a ten-stringed harp. ¹⁰ For you grant victory to kings! You rescued your servant David from the fatal sword ... ¹² May our sons flourish in their youth like well-nurtured plants. May our daughters be like graceful pillars, carved to beautify a palace... May there be no enemy breaking through our walls... ¹⁵ ... Joyful indeed are those whose God is the LORD.

David recognised how fleeting life is (v.4); we are here today gone tomorrow. And returning to his kingly pre-occupation, he prayed for success and then called down God's blessings on his nation.

On a different scale, we can give credit to God for our work skills and the giftings God gives us with which to serve others. And as with Psalm 39, we need to remember daily that we are just guests passing through a brief time of human life with the potential of eternal joy in God.

Poem based on Psalm 144: -

God's the rock who anchors me;
I shine when I trust in him.
My life is short blown like smoke;
From youth to age when eyes grow dim.
He gives me my work and skills;
He gives rest and sets me free,
From worries, fears and ills.
God can take the blows aimed for me.

Prayer: Dear God, I love you Lord. Amen

PSALM 145

The original final two lines of this acrostic psalm of David appear to be lost in antiquity. This sublime psalm invites no further comment.

[1] I will exalt you, my God and King, and praise your name forever and ever. [2] I will praise you every day; yes, I will praise you forever. [3] Great is the LORD! He is most worthy of praise! No one can measure his greatness.

[4] Let each generation tell its children of your mighty acts; let them proclaim your power. [5] I will meditate on your majestic, glorious splendour and your wonderful miracles. [6] Your awe-inspiring deeds will be on every tongue; I will proclaim your greatness. [7] Everyone will share the story of your wonderful goodness; they will sing with joy about your righteousness.

[8] The LORD is merciful and compassionate, slow to get angry and filled with unfailing love. [9] The LORD is good to everyone. He showers compassion on all his creation.

¹⁰ All of your works will thank you, Lord, and your faithful followers will praise you. ¹¹ They will speak of the glory of your kingdom; they will give examples of your power. ¹² They will tell about your mighty deeds and about the majesty and glory of your reign. ¹³ For your kingdom is an everlasting kingdom. You rule throughout all generations.

The Lord always keeps his promises; he is gracious in all he does. ¹⁴ The Lord helps the fallen and lifts those bent beneath their loads. ¹⁵ The eyes of all look to you in hope; you give them their food as they need it. ¹⁶ When you open your hand, you satisfy the hunger and thirst of every living thing. ¹⁷ The Lord is righteous in everything he does; he is filled with kindness. ¹⁸ The Lord is close to all who call on him, yes, to all who call on him in truth.

¹⁹ He grants the desires of those who fear him; he hears their cries for help and rescues them.

²⁰ The Lord protects all those who love him, but he destroys the wicked.

²¹ I will praise the Lord, and may everyone on earth bless his holy name forever and ever.

Poem based on Psalm 145: -

> *Divine God of all creation,*
> *You hear the cry of all,*
> *Who turn to your unfailing love,*
> *And on your mercy call:*
> *Forgive the past of those who turn,*
> *Admit their sin and pray;*
> *Submit their lives to You their king,*
> *And humbly walk your way.*

Prayer: Dear Lord God you keep your promises, you bring justice to the earth, you are righteous in all you do, be my ruler and protector. Amen

PSALM 146

'¹ ... Let all that I am praise the LORD. I will praise the LORD as long as I live. I will sing praises to my God with my dying breath. ³ Don't put your confidence in powerful people; there is no help for you there. ⁴ When they breathe their last, they return to the earth, and all their plans die with them. ⁵ But joyful are those who have the God of Israel as their helper, whose hope is in the LORD their God. ...'

This is true worship – when all that we are is living by God's grace to glorify God's character. We lean into our relationship with God rather than on other people: and then God is not a crutch to support us, but rather the propeller that lifts us into loving service!

⁷ He gives justice to the oppressed and food to the hungry. The LORD frees the prisoners. ⁸ The LORD opens the eyes of the blind. The LORD lifts up those who are weighed down. The LORD loves the godly. ⁹ The LORD protects the foreigners among us. He cares for the orphans and widows, but he frustrates the plans of the wicked. ¹⁰ The LORD will reign forever. He will be your God, O Jerusalem, throughout the generations. Praise the LORD!

These verses are in a similar vein to other passages in the Psalms and to Isaiah 61, where the writer speaks of God proclaiming good news to the poor; comforting the broken-hearted; freeing captives and prisoners; and pouring the oil of joy on people in place of their mourning – God doing all this through the ministry of God's Messiah (The Christ) and by the power of God's Spirit working through God's committed people.

Poem based on Psalm 146: -

God in Christ, open blind eyes,
Save them from all godless lies.
Free the prisoners with good news,
Truth in Christ with hope imbues!
Lift the weary, care for all;
Help the broken to stand tall.
Help us now serve in your power.
On the poor your joy to shower!

Prayer: God be in my hands and feet; God be in my heart and speech! Amen

PSALM 147

¹ ... How good to sing praises to our God! How delightful and how fitting! ² The LORD is rebuilding Jerusalem and bringing the exiles back to Israel. ³ He heals the broken-hearted and bandages their wounds. ⁴ He counts the stars and calls them all by name. ... ⁷ Sing out your thanks to the LORD; sing praises to our God with a harp. ⁸ He covers the heavens with clouds, provides rain for the earth, and makes the grass grow in mountain pastures. ⁹ He gives food to the wild animals and feeds the young ravens when they cry. ¹⁰ He takes no pleasure in the strength of a horse or in human might. ¹¹ No, the LORD's delight is in those who fear him, those who put their hope in his unfailing love.

This psalm of praise to God is one of the last five psalms of the Hebrew Bible which concentrate solely on the congregational praise of God. When we truly praise God, we allow our beings to be flooded with God's grace and goodwill to all the earth.

Although God has provided sufficient for the earth by its ecosystems, humanity has now grown so numerous that our self-focused industry is now rapidly destroying the hand that feeds us. So those who love God must work tirelessly to reverse this trend so that future generations can experience the wonder and joy of the diversity of life and experience Divine relationship through Christ.

^{12} Glorify the LORD, O Jerusalem! ... ^{14} He sends peace across your nation and satisfies your hunger with the finest wheat... ^{19} He has revealed his words to Jacob, his decrees and regulations to Israel... Praise the LORD!

Poem based on Psalm 147: -

Halleluiah! We are truly blessed!
When we listen to his words,
Harmony breaks out and life is best!
God provides for all life and girds
The planet with abundance pressed
His truth reaches out not by swords,
But by those who in his love are dressed!

Prayer: Help us humbly praise your name in all the earth!

PSALM 148

^{1} Praise the LORD from the heavens! Praise him from the skies! ^{2} Praise him, all his angels! Praise him, all the armies of heaven! ^{3} Praise him, sun and moon! Praise him, all you twinkling stars! ^{4} Praise him, skies above! Praise him, vapours high above the clouds! ^{5} Let every created thing give praise to the LORD, for he issued his command, and they came into being. ^{6} He set them in place forever and ever. His decree will never be revoked.

God has created time and space with infinite energy and set within them the laws that necessitated the development of matter and life. These same laws necessitate the degradation of that boundless energy but over such an enduring life time that the Psalmist can poetically declare that creation lasts for ever and ever!

⁷ Praise the LORD from the earth, you creatures of the ocean depths, ⁸ fire and hail, snow and clouds, wind and weather that obey him, ⁹ mountains and all hills, fruit trees and all cedars, ¹⁰ wild animals and all livestock, small scurrying animals and birds, ¹¹ kings of the earth and all people, rulers and judges of the earth, ¹² young men and young women, old men and children.

Love requires action to be real: it is not just cerebral. If we love our Creator, we will praise our Lord God. Inanimate and most non-human life praises God by virtue of being and living out its evolved existence. Humanity and (possibly?) other higher order self-reflecting creatures have the privilege of responding to and living with the Spirit of God and such love needs to be expressed in praise! Hence, we are also susceptible to failure – failure to love God our Creator with all our being.

¹³ Let them all praise the name of the LORD. For his name is very great; his glory towers over the earth and heaven! ¹⁴ He has made his people strong, honouring his faithful ones— the people of Israel who are close to him.

The Psalmist envisages his people (the Israelites) as close to God because of their faithfulness to the revelation of God given through their scriptures. However rose-tinted' the Psalmist is in this psalm, it does reflect the truth that God does work through all who fulfil their true potential by responding to and living out of the love of God in their lives.

A Poem relating to Psalm 148: -

We praise you Lord God our creator,
Divine lover, sustainer, and end,
Both giver of life and redeemer
Divine spiritual guide and our friend!

A prayer: - God, help me meet my full potential with You in life. Amen

PSALM 149

[1] Praise the LORD! Sing to the LORD a new song. Sing his praises in the assembly of the faithful. [2] O Israel, rejoice in your Maker. O people of Jerusalem, exult in your King. [3] Praise his name with dancing, accompanied by tambourine and harp. [4] For the LORD delights in his people; he crowns the humble with victory. [5] Let the faithful rejoice that he honours them. Let them sing for joy as they lie on their beds.

The 'Word of God' is not given by any single verse of Scripture: any one verse needs to be weighed with all other 'scripture' to begin to understand God's character and God's way for us. Besides which, if we hold that scripture is inspired by God's Spirit then we must look to God's Spirit to guide our understanding of it. What was true about 'being glad and rejoicing in the Divine God of Creation' here for ancient Israel, is just as true for all who love the Divine God of all creation today. We need to learn to be glad and seek the joy God can give us in every circumstance of life. As we praise God's character of love especially as revealed through Jesus Christ in the New Testament (Ingil), we will experience God's intimacy even in the midst of tragedy and suffering.

> ⁶'Let the praises of God be in their mouths, and a sharp sword in their hands ⁷to inflict vengeance on the nations and punishment on the peoples ...'

In verse seven, the Psalmist seems to depart from the Word of God given by Moses (Deut. 32 v.35), and as revealed in Jesus Christ and as further called for by St. Paul in the NT (Rom. 12 v.35). In the understanding of the Ancient Israelites, they were called into a covenant relationship with Jehovah God, and this entailed fighting their enemies and bringing about the judgements of God upon them by the sword in battle. However, their prophets gave clear instructions that they were not to be vengeful on their enemies and the same truth holds true today for all people of whatever race or creed: vengeance is not for sinful people but for God alone to execute. Applying verse seven out of the context of the whole of scripture will lead to serious error and sin, whether this is by Christians (witness the Crusades against Muslims in the tenth century) or by Muslims (witness the Jihadi's today believing that murdering 'unbelievers' to be pleasing to Allah).

Poem drawn from Psalm 149: -

Come praise God with your dancing,
With hands and voices do,
Come lift the roof with singing
And smiling faces too!
Live each day with joyful tongue
Gladly face your world
With hope and perseverance
And with faith unfurled!

A prayer: Divine Lord of all, help me follow the way revealed in the sinless life of your coming in Christ Jesus and learn to forgive my enemies and to pray in your character

PSALM 150

¹ Praise the LORD! Praise God in his sanctuary; praise him in his mighty heaven! ² Praise him for his mighty works; praise his unequalled greatness! ³ Praise him with a blast of the ram's horn; praise him with the lyre and harp!

⁴ Praise him with the tambourine and dancing; praise him with strings and flutes! ⁵ Praise him with a clash of cymbals; praise him with loud clanging cymbals. ⁶ Let everything that breathes sing praises to the LORD!

A poem on Psalm 150: -

With your every breath as long as you live
Give praise to the Lord, God the Creator,
Of all life the Author; under all, the Sustain-er:
Of true life the Keeper; In all life, the Wonder,
Let all that has breath, praise God for God's love.
Let all that can sound, give sound to God's praise!
To faith the Provider, near to all, their Redeemer
For all, their true Lover; to faith-life, our Helper.
Praise God – Amen for ever and ever!

A prayer: - I love you Divine Eternal God! Amen

End Notes

Further comment from the Introduction:

These two volumes (part 1 & 2) reflect my personal review of the Psalms of David and are dedicated to all those who are of the 'open and adventurous nature' that I have described, and within the particular monotheistic faiths of Judaism, Islam and Christianity. I doubt it will have any appeal to those of the 'cut and dried nature' within Judaism, Islam or Christianity.

Many of the Psalms have been seen as prophetic by both Jews and Christians pointing forward to the coming of the Jewish Messiah *(a Hebrew name, 'Christos' in Greek and 'Christ' in English)* This specially 'anointed one' was promised by God to Abram in response to his faith in God: God promised him that all the earth's peoples would be blessed through one of his descendants *(Genesis 22 v.18)*. Other Hebrew prophets spoke in terms of God visiting the earth by means of this special Messiah *(e.g., Isaiah 42 v.1-4)*. I shall use the words 'Messiah' and 'Christ' interchangeably to describe this uniquely prophesied person. Christians understand this person as Jesus Christ.

Psalm 76

[2] Jerusalem is where (God) lives; Mount Zion is his home. [3] There he has broken the fiery arrows of the enemy, the shields and swords and weapons of war. This text from verse two is difficult for non-Jews to accept since it implies that God is partial to one nation and one city. However, when looked at in the context of history we can note that the city of Jerusalem (which incorporates Mount Zion) has been over-run and held by various rulers and despots, both secular and religious. And it seems that Almighty God has not overall seen fit to favour that city over any other human city – however one can say it is still there, whereas many other ancient cities have long since gone. The Biblical text makes clear that God has no regards for status and human pride: God looks at the heart!

Psalm 89

In this psalm, Ethan is referring to a prophesy given by Nathan to King David, first written down in 2 Samuel ch.7 and then next recorded in 1 Chronicles ch.17 following the exile to Babylon. Nathan in a vision had received a promise for King David that one of his descendants would build a house (temple) for God and that God would secure his royal throne forever (2 Sam.7 v.16). There was a song-writer by the name of Ethan in the court of King Solomon who may have been commissioned by the King to write a chronicle about his father David, and it is thought by some that his censored account is recorded in the book of Samuel.

Clearly King Solomon took this as a reference to himself and he did build the first temple for God in Jerusalem using the materials his father had collected for that purpose. However, we need to remember to read Scripture in its whole context and it is clear from both the Old and New Covenants, that God does not make unconditional promises (Heb.12 v.22-29). The promises of God are conditional upon our faith and obedience to them. King David and King Solomon took Nathan's prophecy as referring to David's heir Solomon in which case they should have known that David's physical line of earthly kings would not last if they ignored God and turned away from God's grace. And indeed, that is exactly what King Solomon did in his later years and his dynasty did not last.

However, we should also note that the promise of God to King David can be seen in its proper spiritual context as a reference to what God would do through one of David's descendants, the sinless Messiah, Jesus of Nazareth. This was a prophesy similar to that given by God to Abram and again referred not to Abram's earthly descendants (the Jews and the Arabs), but to his one sinless descendant, we now know through Scripture as Jesus the Messiah.

The author of Psalm 89 may or may not have been the same Ethan as lived in King Solomon's time, however I have taken the latter possibility in my brief commentary and that the author was writing in an era when the 'house of David' as an earthly entity had clearly failed. - but I accept it may be that the author may have been a different Ethan

Psalm 96

NT Apostle (prophet) James (Jam.5 v.13) reinforces Psalm 96 with the words: - **'Is anyone suffering, he should pray: is anyone happy, he should sing praises (to God)!'** And an indisputable fact of Christian believers is that they have written more songs and sing God's praises worldwide far more than any other people in history. Why is this? Clearly, they have very good news to share – sins forgiven and a powerful hope of eternal life based on their faith in the death and resurrection of Jesus Christ as the work of Almighty God.

Psalm 110

'Several centuries after the psalms were written, the author to the NT book of Hebrews (writing in about 65 AD) inspired by God's Spirit, quoted psalm 110 to illustrate how Jesus has now been made the perfect spiritual High Priest of our salvation since by raising him from death (following his priestly self-sacrifice), Almighty God had made Jesus a **'priest forever after the order of Melchizedek.' As such Jesus is made far superior to the whole Jewish religious system (Heb.5 v.6).'**

'We can be confident that neither the author of Genesis nor the author of Psalm 110 had any idea that what they were writing about, would be what God's Spirit (through the author of Hebrews) would use in the NT to teach the church about the status and effectiveness of Christ's permanent priesthood. It is by such inspired biblical writing that we can know that God really does communicate with humanity and really did prepare the way for the coming of the world's salvation in Jesus Christ.' – *quoted from my book 'Christian Faith in Today's World', p.12, ISBN 9781983361661*

End Notes

Psalm 2 in similar vein to Psalm 110, speaks of God's particular coming anointed Messiah. It is only Christians and Muslims who accept that Jesus of Nazareth was/is the Jewish Messiah prophesied here and that he is appointed by Almighty God for all time. Christians believe Jesus to be the Word of God become flesh, whereas Islam does not accept that Jesus was/is divine.

Psalm 111 v.9

Isaiah speaks of the coming Messiah as bringing the 'good news of redemption' (Is. 52 v.9) and as God's 'servant' (Is. 52 v.13) who will be 'highly exalted' and would be wounded (52 v14) and who would be 'pieced for our rebellion and crushed for our sins' so we can be 'made whole' and 'healed' (Is.53 v.5 & 6). And (Is 54 v.11) God says by his suffering, his 'servant will make it possible for many to be counted righteous for he will bear all their sins.'

Psalm118 v.22

This OT idiom is quoted five times in the NT (Matt 21v42; Mk 12 v10; Lk 20 v.17; Acts 4v11; 1 Pet.2 v7) referring to the key place Jesus occupies in God's eternal kingdom. The origin of the idiom is lost but the Psalmist uses it in verse 22 and it probably came from a story of an important stone initially discarded at the quarry for the building of the first Hebrew temple. There is also a prophecy in Isaiah (28 v.16) of God laying a cornerstone for a new covenant for people to build on, which was taken as referring to the coming of God's special Messiah. This Isaiah reference is picked up by Paul in NT (Rom.9 v.33) and together with Psalm 118 v22 is used by the NT authors as it fits well with Jesus God's Messiah initially rejected by the Jews and later becoming the cornerstone for our salvation. It is worthy of note that three stones in the temple building can be used to illustrate Jesus' role in God's Kingdom. The cornerstone is the initial foundation stone from which the whole building is set out. The keystone is the final piece of an arch which holds the structure together (bridges God's OT and NT covenants) and a capstone is the final piece of a corner which helps keep two walls in place (cf. Rev.22 v13, quoting Jesus, "I am the Alpha and the Omega, the First and the Last, the Beginning and the End").

Psalm 140

Further to my commentary given for this psalm, I would add that we live in a world where we (together with all life) have to struggle from cradle to the grave in order to develop, create and reproduce and where we undoubtedly meet with suffering: however, I personally do not class the non-human causes of such struggle and suffering as evil, but I accept that you may want to add natural disasters to your definition of evil rather than limit the definition of evil (as I have done in commenting on Psalm 140) to that which shows itself through human minds and deeds.

Philosophers have used such wider definition to oppose the idea that a good Creator God has created a universe where creatures are victims of predation, where natural disasters and diseases cause great suffering, etc. Many Christians have traditionally sought to defend the notion of a Good God, by claiming that the early chapters of Genesis are intended to show that all evil in the universe is the result of human sin. I have written powerfully against this notion on the basis of the clear teaching of Jesus Christ and of the book of Genesis itself *(see Christian Faith in Today's world – Michael Khan).*

End Notes

Printed in Great Britain
by Amazon